SEIZING GOD-GIVEN OPPORTUNITIES

SEIZING GOD-GIVEN OPPORTUNITIES

◆ ◆ ◆

Positioning Yourself To Receive God's Best

by
Jerry Savelle

Harrison House
Tulsa, Oklahoma

Seizing God-Given Opportunities
Positioning Yourself To Receive God's Best
ISBN 1-57794-192-6
Copyright © 1999 by Jerry Savelle
P.O. Box 748
Crowley, Texas 76036

Published by Harrison House, Inc.
P.O. Box 35035
Tulsa, Oklahoma 74153

CONTENTS

◆ ◆ ◆

INTRODUCTION

◆ ◆ ◆

SEIZING GOD-GIVEN OPPORTUNITIES

Once when I was on my way to London to preach in a meeting, I picked up a biography of Henry Ford in the airport bookshop. I like to read autobiographies or biographies of great men and women. And having been in the automotive business before going into the ministry, I especially enjoy reading books about people who are involved in that industry. So I bought this book about Henry Ford to read on the plane. It turned out to be a good investment because it was so inspirational and motivational.

Two Principles

In that book, Henry Ford made two particular statements that led me to the theme of this study.

One of them was this: Henry Ford said that when he was a very young boy, his mother taught him that life would present many opportunities, but it would take self-discipline, courage and perseverance to make those opportunities a reality.

Let me repeat that. *Life will present many opportunities, but it will take self-discipline, courage and perseverance to make those opportunities a reality.*

The second principle Henry Ford's mother taught him was this: A person who says, "I can't," or "I don't want to," will never get anywhere.

Did you get that? *A person who says, "I can't," or "I don't want to," will never get anywhere.*

These two principles lodged deep down in my spirit and in my thinking. I also remembered what the apostle Paul said in 1 Corinthians 16:9 about a door of opportunity opening for him to preach the gospel:

> **For a great door and effectual is opened unto me, and there are many adversaries.**

As I began to meditate on that Scripture, the Holy Spirit led me into this study on seizing God-given opportunities.

CHAPTER 1

◆ ◆ ◆

TAKING POSSESSION OF OPPORTUNITIES SUDDENLY AND BY FORCE

All of us are presented with opportunities every day. Opportunities for greatness. Opportunities for success. And even more importantly, wonderful opportunities to serve God in a greater capacity are given to us every day.

Through this book, God is giving you an opportunity not only to learn more about His Word, but also to better your life. By appropriating what you learn and applying it to your own life and circumstances, you will be able to enjoy a better, more successful life.

God wants your life to be better for His glory. You see, when your life is better—when good things are happening in your life, when you're tapping into greater levels of success and prosperity, when the peace of God is residing within you—it makes God look good. God wants you to seize every opportunity He gives you so that you can make progress in your spiritual life of faith.

SUDDEN FORCE

Since we're using the phrase "seize the opportunity" frequently, I want to define the word *seize* before we go any further. According to Webster's Dictionary, the word *seize* means "to take possession of suddenly and by force or attack or a strike."[1]

Why is it so important to take possession of something suddenly? *Because opportunities do not wait for the faint-hearted, the slow-to-move or cowards.*

Don't Wait for Perfect Conditions

God presents everyone with many opportunities. But before some people will even attempt to seize those opportunities, they want to analyze everything first. They want to reason it all out. They want to make sure all the conditions are perfect before they will act.

If you had waited for all the conditions to be perfect before you bought this book, you probably would never have bought it. If you had waited for all the conditions to be perfect before you went to your last gospel meeting, you probably would never have gone. Most of us wouldn't even get to church on Sunday if we waited for conditions at home to be perfect before we went.

You have to *seize* the opportunity—take possession of it suddenly, by force, by an attack or strike—because opportunities don't wait around for conditions to become perfect. You have to take possession of your opportunities suddenly before they pass you by.

Air Strikes

Taking possession of something by force or a strike reminds me of the television footage of the war in the

---

[1] *Webster's New World College Dictionary. Third Edition. New York: Simon & Schuster, 1996, "seize," p. 1216.*

Persian Gulf. Those bomber and fighter pilots had to strike their targets before the opportunity passed. They had to seize the opportunity to attack before the defenders could put up their defenses.

In the same way, we have to take possession of our opportunities suddenly and forcefully. We have to take hold of opportunities quickly before they pass us by.

God gives everyone opportunities. God doesn't love me any more than He loves you. God doesn't love you any more than He loves someone else.

And that's what I'm going to talk about in the remaining chapters of this book—how to recognize and seize every God-given opportunity that comes your way.

A MATTER OF CHOICE

God gives every person opportunities to hear and respond to His Word. Unfortunately, many do not.

I know people who heard the same Word of Faith message given by Brother Copeland that my wife, Carolyn, and I heard in Shreveport, Louisiana, in 1969. These people sat there and heard exactly the same words we heard. They attended every service we attended. And those folks had exactly the same opportunity *to do something with what they heard* that Carolyn and I had.

And yet, many of those people are doing just as poorly (if not more poorly) today as they were when they heard the message. But Carolyn and I are doing much better. Praise the Lord!

Now, why is that?

Obviously, it wasn't because God was playing favorites. God didn't just set Carolyn and me in that meeting and say,

"They're special. I have a plan for them. The rest of these folks are just allowed to be here. I sent Kenneth Copeland specifically for Jerry and Carolyn Savelle."

No, of course not. That's not what God had in mind. He did send Brother Copeland for us, but He sent him for all the others as well.

There were men and women who sat there and heard what we heard, some of whom had already been to Bible schools. Some of them had been to seminaries. In fact, some of the people who sat in that meeting were already in the ministry.

I hadn't done any of those things. I was just an auto repairman, working on wrecked cars in a paint and body shop.

However, the Word of Faith message changed my life. But many of the other people in that meeting are still living the same way now that they were living then.

Why? What made the difference between those other folks and me?

The difference was that some of those people *did not seize the opportunity to go with God.*

Carolyn and I *chose* to go with God. We *chose* to believe the Word that we heard, and we *chose to put it to work.* Thirty years have come and gone since that time, and because of these choices, God has made our lives better every year.

DRESSED IN OVERALLS

By now some of you may be saying, "Well, I'm not Kenneth Copeland. I'm not Jerry Savelle. I'm not a nationally known preacher. Maybe if I had the opportunities you've had...."

What makes you think you haven't? In fact, before we finish this study, I'll show you a lot of opportunities you've passed by. Why did you pass them by? Why do people fail to seize their God-given opportunities?

Thomas Edison said it best: "The reason many people miss opportunities is because often they [opportunities] come wearing overalls, and they look like work."

If you have a pen handy, you should underline that statement or write it down somewhere so you won't forget it. *The reason people miss opportunities is because they come dressed in overalls, or work clothes, and they look like work.*

Many people want what has happened to others. They want the success others have, but they're not willing to do what others have done to seize the opportunity. They're not willing to do the work.

The Pioneer Spirit

I've always admired pioneers—pioneers in anything, whether it's opening up a new territory, inventing new machines and tools or developing new technology. I love the pioneer spirit.

A lot of people see what pioneers do and wish they were experiencing what the pioneers experience. But they're not willing to have a pioneer spirit.

A pioneer spirit is necessary because someone has to "beat the bushes." Someone has to blaze a trail. Someone has to take the risk of going out and starting a new work in a new place when God gives him or her the opportunity.

Lots of people want to wait until someone else has done all the hard work of starting a new church, and then they come and join when it's finished. (Did I hear some pastors say, "Amen!"?) But those folks are not pioneers. They are the ones who let opportunities pass them by because those opportunities came dressed in overalls and looked like hard work.

Pioneers seize their opportunities. People with the pioneer spirit aren't afraid of the work involved in going with God when He gives them the opportunity to start something new.

"WE NEED PIES"

Let me tell you a true story about a woman who seized an opportunity to become a pioneer and start something new.

During World War II, this woman worked in a delicatessen in Los Angeles. The owner of the delicatessen said to her one day, "Our customers who regularly come here for lunch want pies. At the moment, we don't serve pies at lunch. But we keep getting requests for pies at lunch. So in order to satisfy our customers, I want you to start making pies for lunch."

Now, I'm sure that at the moment her boss told her to start making pies, this woman didn't realize that a wonderful opportunity was being presented to her. She could have let it pass her by. She could have said, "Look, I'm already serving tables. I'm already making hamburgers and sandwiches. I'm already cleaning the tables after the customers leave. I don't need the extra job of making pies. Get someone else to make them."

That's what she could have said. She could have let the opportunity slip by without seizing it. But she didn't. She was willing to work diligently to serve her boss.

Branching Out

So she started making pies, and the customers loved them. In fact, eventually most of the people who came to that delicatessen to eat lunch came because of the pies. And the woman began to realize that if people liked her pies so much, she could start her own pie shop. So she quit her job at the delicatessen and launched out into business for herself making and selling pies.

Of course, it was hard at first. During the first year of being in business for herself, she barely broke even. She was very discouraged and was ready to give up, but her husband said, "No, I don't want you to give up. I believe this is what we're supposed to do. And if I have to quit my job and join in here making pies with you, I'm going to do it. We're going to see this thing through."

So that's what they did. They got the entire family involved, and selling pies became their family's business. It wasn't long before the business began to be successful. By 1964, Marie Callender had 115 pie shops or restaurants in fourteen different states. And in 1986, Ramada Inn, Incorporated bought her pie business for approximately $90 million!

How many of you have eaten a Marie Callender pot pie or dined in a Marie Callender restaurant? Well, you're able to do that because Marie Callender seized an opportunity when God presented it to her, and she worked hard and didn't give up even when the going got tough.

That's the Problem

Now some of you may read the story of Marie Callender's success and say, "Well, I've never been that lucky. Nothing like that ever happens to me."

But how do you know? How do you know you weren't given a similar opportunity?

"Because I don't like making pies!"

That's what I thought.

"Hey, man, it's hard work."

You see, that's your problem. The opportunity showed up wearing overalls, and you didn't want to work. So often we pass up opportunities because we want them to become realities without any effort or confrontation. And we don't want to persevere when the going gets tough.

EVEN THE SNAIL MADE IT

Charles Spurgeon said, "With great perseverance even the snail made the ark."

The other animals, not to mention Noah, were probably ready to give up on him. Can't you just see them all hanging over the rail of the ark, shouting, "Hurry up, slow poke! It's about to rain. Hurry up and get on board so we can shut the door." They were probably impatient, but the snail just kept crawling. And with great perseverance, he made it.

What about you? Are you determined to persevere in what God has called you to do? When an opportunity comes your way, are you so willing to persevere that you'll crawl inch by inch, if you have to, in order to make your dream a reality?

If you are, you can count on the Holy Ghost to supply heaven's power to make certain it will come to pass in your life.

THE FIRST FOUR YEARS

One time I read about a tree called the Chinese Bamboo. Apparently, when you first plant the seed of a Chinese Bamboo tree, you must water and fertilize that seed every day without fail for the first four years. If you don't, it won't grow.

And for the first four years, even if you're watering it and feeding it every day, the growth of the tree is so minimal that it looks as if nothing is happening.

However, during the fifth year that tree grows up to ninety feet!

FIFTH-YEAR RESULTS

But our trouble is that we want the fifth-year results without the four-year application. Isn't that true? We want that accelerated fifth-year growth without persevering through the everyday watering and feeding of the first four years.

Most people want accelerated results before sunset. And when they don't get them, they are ready to give up.

They say, "Well, I'll tell you, this faith lifestyle isn't all that Brother Jerry says it is. I've been living by faith for a week now, and nothing's working. I've even listened to a couple of his tapes and read half of one of his books, but I haven't seen any results. I guess God doesn't intend for it to work for me."

Of course God intends for it to work for you. But it isn't going to work overnight. The ninety-foot growth of the Chinese Bamboo tree doesn't happen during the first year. It takes four years of persistent, daily watering and fertilizing to see the plant *suddenly* shoot up to ninety feet in the fifth year.

Four years of doing something that looks as if it's producing no results and then *suddenly*.... Jesse Duplantis says *suddenly* is his favorite word in the Bible. We all like that word, don't we? We love it when *suddenly* happens. We love to see those spectacular results in short periods of time.

But are we willing to wait? Are we willing to persevere during those first four years? Are we willing to take possession of the opportunity—suddenly and by force—when it first presents itself? And then are we willing to persevere as long as it takes to turn that opportunity into a reality?

CHAPTER 2

◆ ◆ ◆

NOT WITHOUT A FIGHT

As we saw in the last chapter, one reason people miss out on God-given opportunities is that they are not willing to do the work, and they are not willing to persevere. Remember, opportunities do not wait for the faint-hearted, the slow-to-move or cowards. Opportunities must be seized. God-given opportunities rarely wait around for you to analyze every detail and look for perfect conditions before taking possession of them.

But there's another reason people miss out on God-given opportunities: *Many Christians miss opportunities because they're not willing to fight.* They are not willing to contend for their dream. They are not willing to "roll up their sleeves"—spiritually speaking—and go to war for those opportunities.

The Devil Won't Play Dead

Just because God gives you an opportunity for greater service, doesn't mean the devil is going to sit down, roll over and play dead. He is not going to let you seize an opportunity without a fight.

Along with every opportunity comes a confrontation.

The apostle Paul knew that. Let's look at 1 Corinthians 16:9 again:

For a great door and effectual is opened unto me, and there are many adversaries.

Notice that Paul said, **there are many adversaries.** He knew God had given him an opportunity for more effectual service, but he also realized that he wasn't going to be able to seize that opportunity without a fight.

God gives all of us opportunities, but we have to be prepared to fight for them.

WHAT IF...?

The Lord reminded me recently of how important it is to stay prepared to seize and fight for opportunities. He said, "What would have happened if you hadn't been prepared when I gave you the opportunity to purchase that 102 acres of land?"

Those of you who are familiar with my ministry probably have heard my testimony about God blessing us in 1993 with the opportunity to buy 102 acres of land across the road from our ministry headquarters south of Fort Worth. At the time, it was valued at $2.75 million, but God gave us the opportunity to purchase it for $200,000 in cash! He gave us that land so we could fulfill our dream of building a Bible school.

When I think about how God suddenly gave us that opportunity, I wonder, *What if I had not been in position financially to seize that opportunity?* If I hadn't been prepared, or if I had been slow to move, I could have missed the opportunity to purchase $2.75 million worth of property for "a song."

One reason God has been emphasizing to the body of Christ to get its financial affairs in order is so that we can be in position to receive the blessings when they appear. We need to be prepared for the financial inversion that God promised would take place before the appearing of the Lord Jesus. This financial inversion is happening right now. God is putting opportunities into the hands of the body of Christ to obtain what the world thought was theirs but which rightfully belongs to the church. God is giving us opportunities to get it back where it belongs for a "song and a dance."

But if we don't have a song and a dance, we're going to miss the opportunity.

Future Development

Well, fortunately, we were financially prepared to seize the opportunity to buy that 102 acres when it presented itself. We bought that land for the future development of our School of World Evangelism campus so that we could train people in the Word and send them out to evangelize the world.

We made the purchase of this land in 1993, but I thought it was going to be sometime in the distant future before I could build a campus on it. I thought I'd wait until everything was perfect before I'd go any further with the project.

However, God wasn't going to wait for perfect conditions. He said, "Open the school in September of 1994." So we said, "Ok, we'll open it in September." All the while I was thinking, *Lord, why don't You wait until my building is built, the campus is ready and everything is in order? Why can't we wait until all the conditions are perfect?*

But of course I knew I'd never get anything done if I waited until all the conditions were perfect. And besides, I had to obey the Lord. So we announced that the school was starting in September of 1994. We printed brochures and started receiving applications from people from all over the world.

We now had 102 acres of land with no buildings on it and a group of students who were due to come to our school in September. We had a school but no buildings to put it in! Our ministry headquarters building was already overflowing. The auditorium was too small even for our monthly rallies. Every office was crowded, and if we had hired any more people, we would have had to hang them on the walls. There certainly wasn't any room for a school.

But God said, "Start the school in September." So we obeyed God and put things in motion. We started seizing the opportunities.

No "For Sale" Sign

Well, by this time it was May of 1994, and Carolyn and I were getting ready to go to New York to meet some friends before going on to Philadelphia where Jesse Duplantis and I were going to preach. The day before we were to leave, I took some time off and went cruising around the country-side on my motorcycle. I went out on Interstate 35, but I came home on the back roads through the country.

As I came around the corner near our 102 acres, my attention was attracted to the Baptist church less than a quarter of a mile from my ministry headquarters. As I was riding by and glanced at it, the Spirit of God spoke to me and said, "There's your school."

Don't think that God can't talk to you on a Harley! He may have to talk loudly, but He can get through to you. I was just riding by that Baptist church that is just a stone's throw from my 102 acres, and God said to me, "There's your school building I've prepared for you."

However, there wasn't any "for sale" sign on it. And of course I wasn't going to start praying those precious Baptist Christians out of their building. But I knew in my spirit that the Lord wanted that Baptist church building to be my new school building.

"BY THE WAY, DID YOU KNOW..."

Well, I wanted to talk to my wife about what the Lord had said, but by the time she got home, I'd gotten busy with something else, and I didn't mention it.

Then, the next day, we flew to New York where we met Jesse and Cathy Duplantis and some other friends. We toured the city and did some sightseeing.

I kept meaning to call my office manager and ask him to call that Baptist church to see if the building was for sale, but we were so busy I never got a chance to call him. So I thought, *Well, I'll call him tomorrow.*

However, the next day was even busier, and I didn't get time to call him that day either. He was going to meet us in Philadelphia anyway, so I decided I'd just wait until I saw him to tell him about what the Lord had said about the Baptist church.

He was already in Philadelphia by the time we got there. When I checked in, he came up to my room to give me some information about the meeting we were getting ready to conduct. He said, "We've got everybody checked in. Here's the rooming list and the budget for the meeting. And oh, by the way, you know that Baptist church around the corner from us? It's for sale. Do you want it?"

I hadn't even talked to him about it yet! I said, "Yes, I want it." Then I told him what had happened when I had ridden by that church on my motorcycle. I said, "Please call that Baptist pastor right now and tell him I want to meet with him just as soon as I get home."

When we got home, a member of our Board of Directors met us and went over with us to look at that building. The moment I stepped into that church building I thought this building must have been built especially for Jerry Savelle Ministries School of World Evangelism!

The auditorium alone enabled us to triple the number of people we could minister to in our monthly rallies. The education building was perfect for the School of World Evangelism. And on top of everything else, it came with ten acres of land.

Now, that was a God-given door of opportunity. I knew God had arranged it all. So we negotiated a price and bought that building. And we started our School of World Evangelism in September of 1994 just as God had directed us to.

But we wouldn't have been able to do it if we hadn't seized the opportunity when God presented it to us.

AMBITION IS NOT ENOUGH

Every opportunity God gives us demands a steadfast, persevering spirit. Ambition alone is not enough. Many people with ambition never accomplish anything.

To seize an opportunity and bring it to reality, you must be willing to take a risk. You must be willing to lay everything on the line. When you live by faith, times are going to come when you will have to lay everything you have on the line. You must be willing to lose everything in order to seize an opportunity.

You can't hold anything back if you live by faith. So often we say, "I want to live by faith, but I'm not willing to do this or that. I'm not willing to go that far." When you say that, you're making provision for failure.

Ambition—wanting to do it—is not enough. You have to be willing to take risks.

You have to be willing to go out on a limb, trust God and be prepared to fight a good fight.

Real Heroes

Throughout the Word of God, we find men and women who have influenced entire generations. They have influenced entire nations by obeying God, seizing opportunities and turning vision into action.

Hebrews 11 contains the Hall of Fame of men and women of faith in the Old Testament. This chapter reveals the story of people who seized the opportunity to trust God. They were willing to take risks. They were willing to lay their lives on the line. The Bible says some of them even died in faith.

We all want to live in faith. *But are we willing to die in faith?* People who are willing to die in their faith are not afraid to take risks when they know that they have heard from God.

THE KIND WE SHOULD HAVE

Once when Brother Jesse Duplantis and I were in a restaurant, a lady came up to our table and asked if she could take a picture of Brother Jesse to give to her son. She said, "Brother Jesse, you're my son's hero."

What she said really blessed me. Those are the kinds of heroes young people ought to have: people of faith.

You see, society today doesn't know what a hero is. They think somebody who can carry a ball and run 100 yards a game for twelve seasons is a hero. They think somebody who can play a "bad" guitar and shake like a fool and scream words you can't understand is a hero.

Those are not the real heroes. Heroes are people who will not compromise their convictions from the Word of God. Heroes are people who take their convictions and do something to make the world a better place to live in. And while they're seizing their God-given opportunities and turning their vision into action, they help a lot of folks along the way.

Kenneth Copeland is still my hero after all of these years. Oral Roberts is still my hero. These men refuse to compromise the Word of God. They're both still preaching the fundamentals of faith just the way they were when I first heard them in the sixties. (In a meeting recently I was listening to Kenneth Copeland preach, and I leaned over and whispered to Jesse Duplantis, who was sitting next to me, "That's the same message that changed my life when he preached it in Shreveport in 1969." God gave me an opportunity right then to be blessed all over again by that message.)

Consequently, they don't understand what Paul meant when he said, **When I am weak, then am I strong.**

I like to call that strength "Holy Ghost second wind." Paul got his second wind when he was weak. The more his adversaries fought against him, the more he seemed to revel in it. He took pleasure in reproaches, distresses and persecutions for Christ's sake.

THE PRIVILEGE OF SERVING

What was the first thing Paul said in Acts 9:6 while he was still lying in the dust on the road to Damascus blinded by the glory of God? He said, **Lord, what wilt thou have me to do?** He was asking, "What opportunities must I seize for the gospel's sake? What opportunities must I seize to serve You?"

And what was the Lord's answer? He sent Ananias to tell Paul **how great things he must suffer for my name's sake** (Acts 9:16). In other words, Jesus told Paul, "I'm going to give you the privilege of suffering for My name's sake." But He didn't stop there. He supplied Paul with the power to overcome every adversity. He told Paul, **My grace is sufficient for thee: for my strength is made perfect in weakness** (2 Corinthians 12:9). And because Paul knew God's strength was available to him, he knew he could stand firm in any fight.

THE POWER OF PERSISTENCE

Paul loved a good fight, but he knew it took perseverance and persistence to win. He told the Corinthian believers that persistence and perseverance must become habitual.

> Therefore, my beloved brethren, be ye stedfast, unmoveable, always abounding in the work of the Lord, forasmuch as ye know that your labour is not in vain in the Lord.
>
> 1 Corinthians 15:58

Notice the word *always* in that verse. Paul is saying that perseverance can become habitual. But we must realize that if perseverance can become habitual, then quitting can too. For a lot of people, quitting has become a habit. Quitting is part of their character, and they have become natural quitters. If you have developed a habit of quitting, it doesn't take much pressure to get you to quit. But if you can develop a habit of quitting, you can also develop a habit of persevering.

I'm not talking about mind power. I'm not talking about metaphysics. I'm not talking about mind science or even the power of positive thinking. *I'm talking about the power of the Word of God in your heart. I'm talking about faith in your heart and the Word coming out of your mouth.* I'm talking about Holy Ghost power that can make you habitually persistent. Praise God!

God Exalts Persistence

God promotes persistence. He elevates persistent people. Proverbs 22:29 says, **Seest thou a man diligent in his business? He shall stand before kings....** And in Luke 9:62, Jesus warned us, **No man, having put his hand to the plough, and looking back, is fit for the kingdom of God.**

God always says, "Keep going forward. Don't look back." Why? Because the more you look back, the less you can see where God wants you to go. The more you look back, the less you can see of what God has for you up ahead.

In Philippians 3:13, Paul said, **But this one thing I do, forgetting those things which are behind, and reaching forth unto** *those things which are before.* Everything God has for you is ahead of you, not behind you. So stop procrastinating and get moving. Don't wait for perfect conditions before you move out to seize your opportunity. Remember, **If you wait for perfect conditions, you will never get anything done** (Ecclesiastes 11:4 TLB).

Get rid of all of the negative excuses holding you back from seizing the opportunities God has for you. Don't say, "I'm the wrong color," or "I was born on the wrong side of town." When you got born again, you became a new creature and a citizen of the kingdom of God. There's no "wrong side" to the kingdom of God. There's no color barrier there. The Word of God knows no barriers. The Word of God knows no race but one: new creatures in Christ.

Don't say, "Well, I don't have the money." God can get you the money.

Don't say, "I just don't have any creative ideas." God has plenty of creative ideas.

Don't say, "But I don't have the education." The Holy Ghost does. And if He can't teach you, then those folks up at the university certainly can't!

God gives everyone opportunities for more effectual service, but in order to benefit from those opportunities, we have to be willing to take possession of them forcibly when they show up. And we have to be willing to work hard.

Keeman Wilson, the founder of Holiday Inns, was once asked what the key to his success was. His answer was this: "I've worked half days all my life. So I guess my advice to anybody who wants to be successful is just to work half days the rest of your life." Then he added, "It really doesn't matter which half you work—the first twelve hours or the last twelve hours." Keeman Wilson seized an opportunity, and through hard work and perseverance he brought his vision into reality.

All of us can do what the heroes of faith have done. But we have to be willing to work hard and persevere and fight the good fight of faith if we want to bring our God-given opportunities into reality. Opportunities are doors that God opens for us, but as we'll find out in the next chapter, an open door is of no benefit to you unless you're willing to go through it.

CHAPTER 3

◆ ◆ ◆

OPPORTUNITY—AN OPEN DOOR

The apostle Paul called opportunity an open door.

For a great door and effectual is opened unto me, and there are many adversaries.

1 Corinthians 16:9

The Amplified Bible actually uses the word *opportunity* in translating that verse.

For a wide door of opportunity for effectual [service] has opened to me [there, a great and promising one], and [there are] many adversaries.

1 Corinthians 16:9 AMP

What Paul is actually talking about here is an opportunity to preach in Ephesus. Do you remember what he asked the Colossians to pray for him? He asked them to pray that God would open a **door of utterance** for him.

Withal praying also for us, that God would open unto us a door of utterance, to speak the mystery of Christ, for which I am

also in bonds: That I may make it manifest, as I ought to speak.

Colossians 4:3,4

The Amplified Bible says:

And at the same time pray for us also, that God may open a door to us for the Word (the Gospel), to proclaim the mystery concerning Christ (the Messiah) on account of which I am in prison; That I may proclaim it fully and make it clear [speak boldly and unfold that mystery], as is my duty.

Colossians 4:3,4 AMP

When Paul says God has opened a **door of utterance** for him in Ephesus, he means God has given him an opportunity to preach the gospel, an opportunity he hadn't had up to that time. What is a door? A door is an opening, something that gives you access or entry into an area. In Romans 5:2, Paul says our faith gives us access—that is, entry into—grace.

By whom [Christ] **we have access by faith into this grace wherein we stand....**

Faith is the door that gives us access to grace. And that's what an opportunity is. It's a door—an open door.

FOR A PURPOSE

God opened a door of opportunity for Paul in Ephesus. And He opens doors of opportunity for each of us every day. But God doesn't open these doors of opportunity for no reason. The dictionary says an *opportunity* is "a combination of circumstances favorable for a purpose."[1] Pay particular attention to that phrase "for a purpose." Remember, God always has a purpose for what He does.

God gives all of us wide doors of opportunity for effectual service. He gives us opportunities to succeed, to prosper, to make our lives better. He gives those who are in full-time ministry a wider platform from which to preach and teach His Word, just as He did for the apostle Paul in Ephesus. But God's purpose for opening these doors of opportunity is so *that He will be glorified in everything we do.*

God doesn't open doors of opportunity for my greater prosperity and a higher income just so I can buy everything I've ever lusted after. God isn't interested in giving me a bank full of money just so I can squander it on myself. *God wants me to be blessed so that I can be a blessing.* God wants me to be blessed so that I can help others, so that I can be a blessing to other families.

Opportunities begin in the mind of God. They are made available to us every day if we are willing to seize them. But God always has a purpose for giving us each opportunity.

BE READY TO SEIZE THEM

As I said earlier, to seize an opportunity is to take possession of it suddenly and by force. Someone once said that the secret of success is to be ready for the opportunities that come into your life. You can count on it—opportunities won't wait around forever. They must be seized.

---

[1] *Webster's New World College Dictionary, Third Edition.* New York: Macmillan, 1996, p. 950.

They will not wait for the faint-hearted or the slow-to-move. They will not wait for those who are insensitive to them.

God wants us to become more sensitive to the opportunities that are being presented to us. As we saw in Chapter 1, there are many people who will sit in meetings where the Word of God is being preached and do nothing with it. They have the same opportunities to do something with the messages as everyone else, but they don't seize those opportunities.

And yet, there are others who sit in the same meetings, experience the same anointing, hear the same Word, and they seize the opportunity to apply it to their lives. If you examine their lives a year later, you see their lives are better. They have progressed, and the blessing of God is abounding at a greater level in their lives.

However, the lives of the people who did nothing with the message are the same as, or worse than, before.

What's the problem? Is it that God loves one person more than He loves another? Is God going down the row saying, "I love thee. I love thee not?" No, of course not. The difference is that some people seize the opportunity and some do not.

THE REST IS HISTORY

Back in the late sixties, Kenneth and Gloria Copeland and a number of other people who are now in the ministry sat in Brother Kenneth Hagin's meetings where there were just small crowds—about 200 people on the average. They heard Brother Hagin teaching about how to write your own ticket with God. They heard him teach seven steps to prayer that brings results. They heard him teach faith from Mark 11:23-24.

And some of them seized the opportunity to apply that teaching to their lives. When opposition came; when adversity came; when people told them, "This is heresy"; when people told them, "This won't work for you," they just held fast to it. They seized the opportunity, and as the saying goes, "The rest is history." All you have to do is look at their lives today, and you'll see that it works. Praise the Lord!

REEL-TO-REEL

I first came in contact with the Copeland ministry in 1969, so I've been around it almost from the beginning. I've heard what the Copelands preach. I've watched how they conduct their lives. And I can tell you that they haven't changed the message. God has blessed them with a greater capacity, but they're still preaching the same thing today that they preached the first time I heard them in 1969. In fact, in many of his meetings, Brother Copeland still preaches the same message that changed my life thirty years ago in Shreveport, Louisiana.

I have those messages on seven reel-to-reel tapes. (We didn't have cassettes back then.) I still have the big, bulky reel-to-reel tape player I had then. There are fourteen messages on those seven tapes—one on each side. Every so often, God leads me to listen to those tapes again.

When I listen to the message that changed my life, I purposely listen to it as if I have never heard it or anything else about faith before. When I listen to it that way, it always ministers to me exactly the way it did that night in 1969.

One evening while I was listening to that old reel-to-reel tape, I got a telephone call from Brother Copeland.

He said, "What are you doing?"

I said, "I'm listening to you preach."

"What am I preaching?" he asked.

I said, "I'm listening to the tape that changed my life back there in 1969. And you know, Kenneth, this message is still just as anointed as it was the day I first heard it. I feel like I've just been born again tonight."

"Jerry," he said. "Get that tape over here. I need to hear it!"

A Church Full of Folks

When Kenneth Copeland came to Shreveport in 1969, there was a church full of folks who heard that same message. But some of them didn't receive it. In fact, one of the associate ministers sat on the platform and shook his head at everything Brother Copeland said—right in front of everybody. Every person in that church could see him shaking his head, resisting the message, but apparently he didn't care. He didn't believe a word of it.

And he wasn't the only one who refused to believe. This was a large church. There were a lot of people there that night. They heard the same Word of Faith message we heard, but they refused to believe it. They didn't seize the opportunity God had given them.

But Carolyn and I seized that opportunity to take possession of that Word, apply it to our lives, trust God and live by faith. And the rest is history. We seized it, and it worked. Praise God.

Sometimes some of the people who didn't seize this opportunity will say to me, "Oh, Jerry, we see you on television. We've got some of your tapes. We've been reading some of your books. And every time we see you on television, we can't believe you're that same little guy Carolyn used to drag to church, praying you would get filled with the Holy Ghost. We can't believe you're the same guy who was working on wrecked cars and running from God."

Well, the fact is, I'm *not* the same man I was then. The Word I heard that night made a new man out of me. But that's because I seized the opportunity God gave me. Those other people heard the same message, but they didn't seize it. They didn't perceive that God was giving them the same opportunity He was giving me, and they didn't take possession of it. You see, you have to be prepared and sensitive to God-given opportunities because they won't wait for those who are slow to move.

When opportunity knocks, you have to be ready to open the door and walk through it.

LINCOLN WAS READY

Abraham Lincoln once said, "I will study, and I will be ready. And perhaps my opportunity will come." Well, it did. In his early career, Lincoln prepared himself for opportunity. If you read an account of his life before he became President, you'll find out he failed to win public office a number of times. He ran for many offices that he did not win. But he refused to give up. He kept going. He kept preparing himself. He kept studying. He kept himself ready. And when the opportunity came, he seized it. Lincoln has gone down in history as one of the greatest Presidents this nation has ever known. But he wouldn't have been President if he hadn't seized the opportunity when it came.

Lincoln would never have been President if he had waited for all conditions to be perfect before running for the office. Conditions will never be perfect. If I had waited to step out in faith until all conditions were perfect, I would never have done it. Seizing an opportunity always requires faith. Back in 1969, Carolyn and I had to make a decision to step out in faith to fulfill the call of God on our lives. We said, "We don't know a whole lot about where we're headed, but we do know we're called, and we're going to fulfill that call."

"Don't Go!"

God told me to shut my business down and to spend the next three months in the back bedroom of my house listening to those seven reel-to-reel tapes, reading the Bible that Brother Copeland had given me with all of his own study notes in it and preparing myself to preach the Word of God.

A lot of Christian people around me then were trying to ship me off to a Bible college. And I was willing to go. In fact, I said, "I'll go." But the Lord kept saying to me, "Don't go." And I'd tell these folks, "But the Lord doesn't want me to go to Bible college."

"Why not?"

"Well," I'd say, "He said He just doesn't have four years for me to waste."

"But how can you be a preacher if you don't go to Bible school?"

"I don't know," I'd say. "I'm not arguing with you. All I know is what I believe God said to me."

Then they'd say, "How could you know what God said? You're too young in this. You've only been in this for six months. God won't talk to you. He talks to us."

But I knew God had said, "Don't go."

CARBON COPIES

Some of these people actually got angry that I wouldn't take their advice and go to Bible school. But I didn't go. The Holy Ghost said, "If *I* can't teach you, I know that bunch at the Bible college can't." Of course, I know God hasn't said that to everyone who has desired to go to a Bible school. But He did say it to me.

You have to understand that there were no Word of Faith Bible schools then. There was no Rhema Bible Training Center then. If I had gone to the Bible college these people wanted me to go to, I would have come out as a carbon copy of everyone else who came out of that Bible college. I knew people who had gone to that Bible school who weren't even in the ministry. They were selling life insurance, selling shoes and driving trucks because they hadn't been able to make it in the ministry. They weren't able to make it in the ministry because they had very little revelation knowledge.

They knew a lot *about* the Bible, but they didn't *know* how to do the Bible.

"PUT ME DOWN, AND I'LL TELL YOU!"

One time one of these people came up to me after he had graduated from four years of Bible college. Now when this fellow had left for Bible school, I was just an auto repairman. But by the time he came back, I had surrendered my life to God and was flowing in the ministry. And God was working miracles in the streets in our soul-winning meetings.

This man grabbed me by the lapels of my coat, practically dragged me off my feet and yelled, "What's the difference between you and me? I've spent the last four years of my life preparing for the ministry. But I'm selling insurance while you're out here doing what I went to Bible school to learn how to do! Why?"

I said, "Put me down, and I'll tell you!"

Well, he let go of my coat, and I said to him, "The difference between you and me is that you know a lot *about* the Bible, but I'm out *doing* the Bible."

And that was exactly what the difference was. This man could tell you what clothes Paul wore when he wrote the letter to the Ephesians. He could tell you the hours of the day John slept on the Isle of Patmos between revelations. But I could tell you how to do what Paul and John said, because I was out doing it. Praise God. I had seized the opportunity to put it into practice.

THE OTHER 999

God presents to us every day greater opportunities to serve Him, to make our lives better, but if we are insensitive to those opportunities, we may let them slip by. If you are insensitive, if you're caught up in a problem, if you're caught up in negativism, you may not recognize the opportunities God is placing before you. God may open a door, but you won't notice it or you'll refuse to go through it.

Many people only recognize opportunities when they see someone else doing something first. Then they wish they had done that. Have you ever said, "I wish I had thought of that"? That means you only recognized the opportunity after you saw someone else seizing it. "I wish I'd thought of that. I wish we were doing that. I wish I'd thought to do that in our ministry. I wish I'd been given that idea."

Well, how do you know you haven't? God may have given you that opportunity, but because you were insensitive, you missed it.

Smith Wigglesworth once said, "God will pass over a thousand men to find *one* with faith."

That doesn't mean those other 999 men didn't have the same opportunity. They may have had the same opportunity, but God couldn't find any faith in them.

Here's a sobering thought: Happy Caldwell—who, besides being a pastor and teacher, owns a Christian television station in Little Rock, Arkansas—once said to me that God told him that he was not His first choice among people to do what he is doing in his city. God said He had spoken to other men before He spoke to Happy about what he is presently doing. But either out of fear or lack of discipline or disobedience or insensitivity to the Spirit, these other men wouldn't do it. But Happy Caldwell seized the opportunity when God presented it to him. He saw an open door of opportunity, and he was willing to enter into it by faith.

I don't want somebody else seizing my opportunity. Therefore, I want to be more sensitive to the opportunities and the open doors that God presents in my life. I want to be ready to step through those open doors by faith and seize my opportunities to serve God in a greater capacity.

CHAPTER 4

◆ ◆ ◆

SEEING THROUGH THE ADVERSITY

There is another reason besides insensitivity and lack of preparation that makes people fail to seize their God-given opportunities. Sometimes people don't step through the doors God opens in their lives because they don't see the opportunity behind the adversity that comes with it.

Remember, the apostle Paul said every door of opportunity is attended by adversaries.

For a great door and effectual is opened unto me, and there are many adversaries.

1 Corinthians 16:9

Adversaries bring adversity, that is, opposition, and as we found out in chapter 2, the devil is not going to let you seize your opportunities without a fight.

The biggest difference between the people who seize their God-given opportunities and those who don't is that the man or woman of faith can see an opportunity in every adversity. Even though every opportunity has adversity with it, the man or woman of faith doesn't focus on the adversity, but only on the opportunity behind it.

WHAT REALLY MADE DAVID KING

Let me give you an example from the story of David and Goliath. If you ask the question "Who made David king of Israel?" most people will say, "God made David king." Well, it's true that God *chose* David to be king after He had rejected King Saul (1 Samuel 16), so we know God was behind the whole thing. But what really made David king was his confrontation with Goliath.

David didn't enter into the kingship until after he had fought and defeated Goliath. His adversity was in reality an opportunity for promotion.

And David left his carriage in the hand of the keeper of the carriage, and ran into the army, and came and saluted his brethren. And as he talked with them, behold, there came up the champion, the Philistine of Gath, Goliath by name, out of the armies of the Philistines, and spake according to the same words: and David heard them. And all the men of Israel, when they saw the man, fled from him and were sore afraid. And the men of Israel said, Have ye seen this man that is come up? surely to defy Israel is he come up: and it shall be, that the man who killeth him, the king will enrich him with great riches, and will give him his daughter, and make his father's house free in Israel. And David spake to the men that stood by him, saying, What shall be done to the man that killeth this Philistine, and taketh away the reproach from Israel? for who is this uncir-

cumcised Philistine, that he should defy the armies of the living God?

...And Saul said to David, Thou art not able to go against this Philistine to fight with him: for thou art but a youth, and he a man of war from his youth.

1 Samuel 17:22-26,33

What happened there? David seized an opportunity. All of his brothers and the rest of the army of Israel saw only adversity. They saw only an adversary who seemed too big to overcome. But although David saw the adversary, by faith he looked past him to the opportunity. He realized that adversity is an opportunity for greatness, an opportunity to excel, an opportunity to go further than ever before. Praise the Lord.

David saw past what looked like sure defeat to the opportunity behind it. He demonstrated that, through faith and perseverance, you can achieve success out of what seems to be destined for failure. The very thing that others are failing at can become the foundation for your success.

But you have to persevere, and you have to be willing to fight.

FINDING JOY IN THE GOOD FIGHT OF FAITH

Both David and Paul demonstrated that when you are truly determined to win, you can actually find joy in overcoming obstacles. Can you imagine that? Can you imagine persevering to the point that it actually becomes fun to fight the good fight of faith?

Now, I didn't start saying this right away, but as I persevered and progressed in my faith walk, I got to the point that I started saying to the devil, "I just want you to know you're giving me another preaching story. You ought to know me by now—I'm not going to quit. I'm not going to give up. I might get knocked down, but you know, devil, one of my favorite Scriptures is Micah 7:8: **When I fall, I shall arise.** Even when you knock me down, I will get back up. I'll brush myself off and just keep standing and standing. And you know that God has honored it. He's given me victory before, and I intend to win this one too.

"So, devil, I just want you to know that this adversity, this opposition, this thing you're calling impossible is soon going to be another testimony and a preaching story. I suggest you quit now, or when I win, I'm going to tell everybody in the body of Christ how I did it."

That's how you talk when it becomes a joy to fight the good fight of faith.

THE JOY OF BELIEVING

The apostle Paul was totally different than most Christians today because he talked about the *joy* of believing. Unfortunately, you hear Christians today saying things like, "We have to use our faith *again?* Has it come to this? How long will it take this time? I hope I don't have to use my faith again for at least six months. This last project almost killed us!"

But Paul enjoyed living by faith. That's the reason he said he wouldn't die until he had finished his course. He told the Philippian church he couldn't leave until he had taught them the joy of believing.

> **For to me to live is Christ, and to die is gain. But if I live in the flesh, this is the fruit of my labour: yet what I shall choose I wot not. For I am in a strait betwixt two, having a desire to depart, and to be with Christ; which is far better: Nevertheless to abide in the flesh is more needful for you. And having this confidence, I know that I shall abide and continue with you all for your furtherance and joy of faith.**
>
> **Philippians 1:21-25**

In effect, Paul was saying, "I'm having a hard time making a decision here. Personally, I'd rather die and thus fulfill my ultimate goal by going on to be with the Lord, but I've chosen to live because you need me. And I want to teach you the joy of believing."

Paul felt he could not die yet, because the body of believers he had been entrusted with had not yet realized the joy of believing or the joy of faith.

There is a joy in believing. There is a joy in standing. There is a joy in being patient. There is a joy in persevering. But you'll never know it if you are prone to quit. You'll never know that joy if you always break under pressure.

What others say is destined to fail can, with great perseverance, be turned into a great victory in your own life. When you are truly determined to win, you can actually find joy in overcoming obstacles.

NOT KNOWING WHEN TO QUIT

Paul was a success because he refused to quit. Acts 13 describes a time when Paul seemed to be in a position every preacher would like to be in.

49

> And the next sabbath day came almost the whole city together to hear the word of God.

Acts 13:44

Almost the whole city came to hear Paul preach the Word. (Don't you know that has to make a preacher's heart happy? Imagine what it would be like if everyone in your city came to hear the gospel preached!) Talk about a wider platform. Talk about an open door of opportunity. Paul saw here an opportunity to affect more lives than ever before. But what happened? Along with the opportunity came adversity and adversaries.

> **But when the Jews saw the multitudes, they were filled with envy, and spake against those things which were spoken by Paul, contradicting and blaspheming. Then Paul and Barnabas waxed bold, and said, It was necessary that the word of God should first have been spoken to you: but seeing ye put it from you, and judge yourselves unworthy of everlasting life, lo, we turn to the Gentiles. For so hath the Lord commanded us, saying, I have set thee to be a light of the Gentiles, that thou shouldest be for salvation unto the ends of the earth. And when the Gentiles heard this, they were glad, and glorified the word of the Lord: and as many as were ordained to eternal life believed. And the word of the Lord was published throughout all the region.**

Acts 13:45-49

Notice what was happening here. The Word of God was impacting an entire region. But just as things seemed to be going well, opposition showed up.

> But the Jews stirred up the devout and honourable women, and the chief men of the city, and raised persecution against Paul and Barnabas, and expelled them out of their coasts. But they shook off the dust of their feet against them, and came unto Iconium. And the disciples were filled with joy, and with the Holy Ghost.

Acts 13:50-52

Just as Paul and Barnabas seemed to be having great success, adversaries came and expelled them from the city. But did these adversaries steal their joy? No. Paul and Barnabas found joy in overcoming obstacles. There was a joy present in their lives even in the midst of adversity. There was joy even in the midst of opposition. Why? Because they were determined to seize and fulfill the opportunity God had given them.

I suggest you write the following statement down somewhere so you won't forget it. *People become successful because they don't know when to quit.*

The word *quit* is not in the vocabulary of winners. For winners like Paul and Barnabas, quitting was not an option. Paul and Barnabas weren't discouraged by adversity. They didn't quit when they encountered opposition. They just shook the dust of that town off of their feet and went on to the next one.

Not Without the Ability

God never gives us an opportunity without first giving us the ability to achieve it. So stop making excuses. Let go of negatives.

"I'm not educated enough."

The opportunity would never have come to you if God hadn't already given you the ability to achieve the goal. And apparently, your education or lack of education didn't have anything to do with it. Otherwise the opportunity would not have been given to you.

"Yeah, but I was born on the wrong side of town." That's not the way God thinks.

"Well, I was born poor." That's not the way God thinks.

"Yeah, but I'm of the wrong race."

God doesn't care about any of those things. God gives opportunity with no boundaries, no restrictions. God-given opportunity is not limited by education. It's not limited by financial status. It's not limited by racial prejudice. God gives opportunities to everyone, and He gives the ability to achieve them.

It is said that Thomas Edison failed 32,000 times before he perfected the reproduction of the human voice in what he later called the phonograph. He failed 32,000 times! But he didn't give up. He didn't quit. He stayed in his laboratory until he got it done. He persevered.

Some Christians never stay with something long enough to overcome the adversity that comes with the opportunity. They say, "I confessed three times that I'm healed, but nothing happened. This stuff doesn't work."

"Well, I tithed twice, and no windows have opened to me."

If Thomas Edison had quit that soon, he would never have reached his goal. He failed 32,000 times, but he got up and tried one more time—and that time he got it right. Praise the Lord.

TAP INTO IT

Henry Ford once said, "There is no man living who cannot do more than he thinks he can do."

I'm a sports enthusiast. I enjoy watching sports of all kinds. One of the things I enjoy about sports is watching people excel. I love to watch people striving for perfection. I love the discipline, the perfection, the striving to go further than anybody else has. When we see a great athlete excelling at some sport like gymnastics or track and field, we sometimes tend to dismiss their achievement by saying, "Oh, he or she was just born with that ability." But how many other people were also "born with" that kind of talent but didn't succeed because they never tapped into it?

I'm speaking here from personal experience. I really believe that if I had tapped into a talent I was apparently born with, I could have been a musician. I love music. I have a phenomenal memory for the lyrics and tunes of songs. I remember songs I heard years ago. All anyone has to do is hum or whistle a tune from some song, and I can tell you what song it is and who recorded it.

When I was a young boy, my sister, who is not quite four years younger than I am, decided she wanted to take piano lessons. So she persuaded our parents to buy her a piano and to send her to a piano teacher. She'd come home from piano class and play the tunes she learned. I'd hear her picking out those pieces of music, and later, when no one was looking, I would slip into the living room and pick out the same tunes on the piano.

But I had a friend named Kenny who lived across the street from me who was the same age I was. One day

Kenny caught me playing the piano. And he called me a "sissy." He said that boys who play the piano are sissies. Well, we fought all over the living room, out into the front yard and all the way to his house. And I never touched that piano again because I was *not* going to have Kenny calling me a sissy. I allowed his taunting me to keep me from tapping into a gift I still believe I had.

However, while I was out proving to a neighbor boy that I wasn't a sissy, people like Jesse Duplantis were learning to play piano, to play guitar, to write songs. When Jesse Duplantis taps into his gift, it blesses people. When I try to tap into that gift, what comes out sounds like a prophecy in tongues! Anyone hearing it would have to pray for the interpretation! You wouldn't think I have any musical talent at all, because I didn't tap into it years ago. I didn't seize the opportunity to develop it when I had the chance.

PEOPLE OF GREAT PASSION

How many opportunities do you suppose you've let slip by? How many opportunities do you suppose God has presented to you just in the last year? How many opportunities to progress to a higher level have slipped by because you weren't willing to make changes, you weren't flexible, you were secure in the old way of doing things? Or because you had a fear of failure? Or you were afraid of what someone else might think?

How many God-given opportunities do we let slip by because they come wearing overalls and look like too much work?

Opportunities become realities only to people of great passion. They become realities only to people who refuse to give up even when facing overwhelming odds.

Albert Einstein said, "Only the one who devotes himself to a cause with his whole strength and soul can be a true master. For this reason, mastery [or success] demands all of a person."

To seize an opportunity, you have to put your all into it. When God gives a vision, you have to put your all into it.

For instance, when God calls you into ministry, you have to put your all into it. You really can't do something else on the side. Now, you may do something else part-time while you're preparing for full-time ministry. I still repaired cars on the side while God was teaching me. God blessed me and kept food on our table and the electric bills paid through my ability to repair wrecked automobiles during the time I was preparing for the ministry.

But there finally came a time when the ministry sustained me. I no longer work on wrecked cars on the side to provide income for the ministry. If I work on a wrecked car now, it's because I like to restore classic cars as a hobby.

Do you understand what I'm saying? To seize an opportunity, you have to be willing to put your all into it. Progress is never achieved by people who have no passion. Progress is never achieved by people who refuse to press on in spite of adversity and opposition.

PAUL WOULDN'T STAY DEAD

The apostle Paul was so passionate about preaching the gospel that he refused to stay dead when his adversaries stoned him! The Bible tells us that in Lystra his opponents actually dragged him out of the city, stoned him and left him for dead.

And there came thither certain Jews from Antioch and Iconium, who persuaded the people, and, having stoned Paul, drew him out of the city, supposing he had been dead. Howbeit, as the disciples stood round about him, he rose up, and came into the city: and the next day he departed with Barnabas to Derbe. And when they had preached the gospel to that city, and had taught many, they returned again to Lystra, and to Iconium, and Antioch, Confirming the souls of the disciples, and exhorting them to continue in the faith, and that we must through much tribulation enter into the kingdom of God.

Acts 14:19-22

The religious Jews were so upset with Paul that they drew him out of the city and stoned him. They left him for dead. Now that's about the time most folks would give up on seizing the opportunity!

But not Paul. He was not finished. Even dead, he was a man of great passion. He would not stay dead until he was satisfied he had finished his course.

Paul would not stay dead. He got right back up and went back into the city and preached there! Now if most preachers today were stoned in a certain city, they would avoid that city at any cost. They would never go there again. There are cities in the United States that I've heard certain preachers describe as "preachers' graveyards." They say "You can't have revival there." Well, I think we should go there to preach anyway just to prove the devil wrong.

And that was Paul's attitude. Paul was a man of great passion, and he wouldn't quit until he finished his course. You can't keep success-minded people down.

THE NOSE OF THE BULLDOG

People of faith cannot be kept down. They will rise to the occasion every time. Notice that Paul didn't live his life in a defensive mode. He was on the offense. He was aggressive in his faith.

People who live defensively never rise above their circumstances. Being on the offense is the key that unlocks the door to making God-given opportunities a reality.

Winston Churchill said, "The nose of a bulldog is slanted backwards so he can continue to breathe without letting go." That's perseverance. When a bulldog latches onto something, he refuses to let go until his goal has been reached. And his nose is designed to allow him to keep breathing without letting go.

I don't care what you're involved in and how difficult it may seem—the Holy Ghost will keep pumping heavenly air into your lungs if necessary so you won't have to give up until you have finished your course. When God says stand and **having done all, to stand** (Ephesians 6:13), He means for you to keep standing. And He will supply you with breath while you are standing so you won't have to let go.

CONFIDENCE, COURAGE, CONVICTION, CONSTANCY

Hebrews 12:1 says, **Let us throw off everything that hinders and the sin that so easily entangles, and let us run with perseverance the race marked**

out for us (NIV). And Galatians 6:9 exhorts us, **Let us not become weary in doing good, for at the proper time we will reap a harvest if we do not give up** (NIV).

At the proper time you will reap a harvest. The greatest rewards you'll ever know come only when you have stood fast on the Word of God and refused to quit.

You can seize your God-given opportunities if you have *confidence,* you have *courage,* you have *conviction* and you are *constant.*

When God gives you a vision, don't let go of it. Write it down. Keep it before your eyes so you'll always be headed in the right direction.

What is your goal?

What is your vision?

What is your objective?

Write your goals and objectives down and keep them before you so you will not lose direction even in the midst of adversity. As the Lord said to the prophet Habakkuk,

> **Write the vision, and make it plain upon tables, that he may run that readeth it. For the vision is yet for an appointed time, but at the end it shall speak, and not lie: though it tarry, wait for it; because it will surely come, it will not tarry.**
>
> **Habakkuk 2:2,3**

CHAPTER 5

◆ ◆ ◆

A CHANGE OF ATTITUDE

B y now we have discovered a number of reasons why people don't seize their God-given opportunities. We discovered that often people miss an opportunity because they're insensitive to it, because they are unprepared for it, because they focus on the adversity rather than the opportunity or because they are not willing to work.

Some people think everything should be handed to them on a silver platter and that the world owes them a living. They want conditions to be perfect before they move. They are looking for security, and they are unwilling to take risks.

STICK YOUR NECK OUT

But we've already found out from the Word of God that **he that observeth the wind shall not sow; and he that regardeth the clouds shall not reap** (Ecclesiastes 11:4). Or as *The Living Bible* paraphrases it, **If you wait for perfect conditions, you will never get anything done.**

To turn an opportunity into a reality, you must be willing to stretch yourself. You must aim high. *And you must be willing to take risks.*

Security and opportunities very seldom run together. Too often we want to be able to hold onto what we have, to what we feel secure in, before we are willing to step out and seize an opportunity. But as we've already learned, opportunities seldom wait around for the faint-hearted and the slow-to-move.

Someone once said, "Even a turtle doesn't get ahead unless he's willing to stick his neck out." In order to step through an open door of opportunity that God has given you, you have to be willing to give up your security and take a risk.

In Luke 9:23-24 Jesus said, **If any man will come after me, let him deny himself, and take up his cross daily, and follow me. For whosoever will save his life**—there's that security people like to hang onto—**shall lose it: but whosoever will lose his life for my sake, the same shall save it.**

What Jesus is really saying here is that in order to follow Him, in order to be His disciple, you have to take a risk. You have to stretch yourself. You have to let go of what you feel is security, because security and opportunity seldom run together. In order to seize an opportunity, you have to "stick your neck out," take a risk and lay hold on it by faith.

THEY NEVER GOT OUT OF THE BOAT

The only way to seize a God-given opportunity is by faith. *If an undertaking does not demand an application of faith, then it's probably not from God.*

Everything God asks us or tells us to do is impossible in the natural. If it were possible in the natural, it wouldn't take any faith. But the Bible says it is impossible to please God without faith (Hebrews 11:6).

So if you're doing something that doesn't require any faith, quit doing it and get over into the supernatural. Listen to God about the things men will say are impossible because the things men say are impossible, God says are possible!

Have you ever stretched yourself? Have you ever taken a risk? Were you told you were a fool for doing it? Did a bunch of self-proclaimed experts come around telling you, "You cannot walk on water"?

But they've never gotten out of the boat themselves, so how would they know you can't walk on water? Particularly if God is telling you to do it? Jesus didn't tell Peter he couldn't walk on water (Matthew 14:29), but in order to do it, Peter had to take the risk of getting out of the boat.

WE JUST LOADED UP THE CAR

When Carolyn and I made up our minds to surrender our lives to full-time ministry, we had to take a risk. It was tempting to think, *Well, as soon as we get out of debt and have a little money in the bank for a little security, we can step out and live by faith.* But, of course, that day would probably never have come. If we had waited for conditions to be perfect, we would never have done what God was calling us to do.

Conditions at the time were certainly not perfect. But Brother Copeland had asked me to come to Fort Worth and go to work for him in his ministry. In the natural, it didn't look like the thing to do. But we knew in our spirits that it was the will of God. And we had made up our minds that we were going to step out in faith, take the risk and obey God. In order to seize the opportunity to go into full-time ministry, we had to just load up the car and go!

And we did. We loaded up our old 1964 Oldsmobile "luxury sedan," which had long since lost its "luxury." Everything we owned was in that car and a little U-Haul trailer. And all we had was junk. Some of our stuff blew out of the trailer on Interstate 20 between Shreveport and Fort Worth, and I was so ashamed of it, I wouldn't even turn around and go back to pick it up. I just left it lying in the road.

PRAYING PAYDAY IN

When we got to Fort Worth, the only house we could find that we could afford to rent was a tiny little wood frame house that was owned by a student at the Baptist seminary. And he couldn't afford to repair it, so you know what that house looked like! I think we moved into that house just before the city would have come to put a sign saying "condemned" in the front yard. One time my mother-in-law got locked in the bathroom because the doorknob fell off the door. That's the kind of shape that little house was in.

As if this weren't enough, the first day I arrived at Brother Copeland's office to go to work, his opening remarks to me were, "In the natural, I can't afford you. If you ever get paid, it will be because you used your faith." Man, that's just what you want to hear from your new employer, isn't it?

Well, I didn't worry too much about it at first. It had taken faith to get us this far. So I assumed faith could keep us going. But sure enough, the first time payday came around, it appeared that I wouldn't get paid.

And Brother Copeland said, "I told you you'd have to use your faith if you got paid. Are you praying?"

I said, "Yes, sir."

"Then don't let up," he said. "The day isn't over yet. Keep praying."

Well, I went back to my "office." Actually, it was just a hallway where I had installed some shelves and tape duplicating machines. But that day, that hallway became my "wailing wall"! I tell you, I bound everything that could be bound. I loosed everything that could be loosed. I prayed. I agreed. I confessed. I fasted. I did everything I'd ever been taught to do.

And before the day was up, we got paid! Hallelujah. In fact, Brother Copeland told the bookkeeper, "Wait until the last minute to pay Jerry. Don't let him know we've gotten the money. Let him pray next payday in too."

Every Demon in Hell

I'd leave Brother Copeland's ministry office, get in my old car, crank it up and watch the smoke billowing out of it. It sounded like a threshing machine. I'd have to hang my head out the window to see when the traffic light changed. You couldn't see it for the smoke.

Then I'd pull up in front of our dump of a house. It looked like every demon in hell was ganged up in the front yard. It seemed like they were waiting to welcome me home with words like, "You'll never leave here. This is as far as you'll ever go. We're going to kill you here."

But we kept on living by faith. We believed God was giving us opportunities to be in His perfect will for the first time in our lives. And we began seizing those opportunities.

And as we did, God began to bless us. He began to promote us. He began to work in our lives. Of course, it didn't happen overnight. It didn't happen in a month. It didn't happen in a year. But things began to happen. We continued to stand on the Word of God, continued to stretch ourselves, continued to take the risk of believing God—and we've been doing it ever since. And God has honored our faith and blessed us. Praise God.

A Matter of Perspective

God has given you world-overcoming faith. He has given you a faith that is capable of seizing every opportunity. Often, turning an opportunity into a reality looks so impossible that it keeps you from even making an effort to seize the opportunity at all. But if you don't make an effort, there's no way to succeed.

Whether you make that effort depends on your point of view. It depends on how you view opportunities. Whether you seize an opportunity or not is a matter of perspective.

Some people seem to have the wrong perspective on things. They look at every little hill of adversity as a huge mountain that's impossible to climb. But the minute you begin to think something is impossible, you have given the devil all the ground he needs to defeat you. The moment the devil realizes you're viewing something as impossible to achieve, he'll keep you up all night reminding you how you're bound to fail if you even try to do whatever it is. He'll remind you of how impossible this thing is.

But in reality, if it were impossible, God wouldn't have given you the opportunity and wouldn't have given you the ability beforehand to accomplish it. Remember, God never gives an opportunity without first giving the ability to seize it and accomplish it.

Jesus would never tell us to cast out devils if He hadn't first given us the authority and the ability to do it. He wouldn't tell us to heal the sick if He had not first given us the authority and the ability and the power to do it. God never asks you to do something unless He first gives you the ability to do it. But you have to tap into that ability and appropriate it by faith.

Forgetting Their Covenant

Let me give you an example from the Bible of how your perspective can affect your outcome. Your perspective can make the difference between victory and defeat.

We looked at part of the story of David's victory over Goliath in an earlier chapter, but let's look at it again for a moment. I want you to notice something at the beginning of the story that has a direct bearing on the outcome.

At the beginning of 1 Samuel 17 we find the armies of Israel under the command of King Saul engaged in war with the Philistines.

> **Now the Philistines gathered together their armies to battle, and were gathered together at Shochoh, which belongeth to Judah, and pitched between Shochoh and Azekah, in Ephesdammim. And Saul and the men of Israel were gathered together, and pitched by the valley of Elah, and set the battle in array against the Philistines. And the Philistines stood on a mountain on the one side, and**

Israel stood on a mountain on the other side: and there was a valley between them.

And there went out a champion out of the camp of the Philistines, named Goliath, of Gath, whose height was six cubits and a span.

1 Samuel 17:1-4

The army of the Philistines was on one side of the valley and the army of Israel on the other. And every day Goliath, the gigantic warrior champion of the enemy army, came out and challenged the men of Israel.

And he stood and cried unto the armies of Israel, and said unto them, Why are ye come out to set your battle in array? am not I a Philistine, and ye servants to Saul? choose you a man for you, and let him come down to me. If he be able to fight with me, and to kill me, then will we be your servants: but if I prevail against him, and kill him, then shall ye be our servants, and serve us. And the Philistine said, I defy the armies of Israel this day; give me a man, that we may fight together. When Saul and all Israel heard those words of the Philistine, they were dismayed, and greatly afraid.

...And all the men of Israel, when they saw the man, fled from him, and were sore afraid. And the men of Israel said, Have ye seen this man that is come up?...

1 Samuel 17:8-11,24,25

Notice what it was about Goliath that frightened the men of the army of Israel. It was *what they saw* that frightened them. It was the way they viewed Goliath, that is, the perspective they had of him, that made them afraid. Now don't misunderstand me. In the natural there was cause to be afraid. This man was a certified champion. He was huge, and he was armed with huge weapons. He had a long list of victories on his resume, so to speak. From the natural point of view the men of Israel had every right to be afraid of him.

But the men of Israel had forgotten something very important. They had forgotten that they were the army of God. They had forgotten that they were a covenant people. Their fear had caused them to forget that God had already promised that when their enemy came against them one way, He would cause him to flee seven ways (Deuteronomy 28:7). God had already told them that **the Lord, he it is that doth go before thee; he will be with thee, he will not fail thee, neither forsake thee: fear not, neither be dismayed** (Deuteronomy 31:8).

God had promised the children of Israel that He was always on their side, and they should have remembered that **God is not a man, that he should lie** (Numbers 23:19). But when they saw what appeared to be an impossible situation, they took the wrong perspective. Their fear made them forget everything they had been taught.

AN ATTEMPT TO STEAL THE WORD

How many of us have had this same kind of experience? We've gone to believers' conventions or camp meetings or even to churches where we received revelations from the Word of God—but the minute we got home, we were faced with some crisis or some stiff opposition that made us forget everything we had just learned.

What happened? Just what Jesus said would happen: **Satan cometh immediately, and taketh away the word that was sown in their hearts** (Mark 4:15).

So the crisis or the adversity you may experience after leaving a meeting or even after you finish reading this book is an attempt of the devil to steal the Word the Holy Spirit has sown in your heart. If Satan attacks you immediately, it's a sign that what you heard or read is a threat to him.

But when that attack comes, don't do what the men of the army of Israel did. Don't forget everything you know about your covenant. Lay hold of the Word you heard or read, apply it and stand on it. Either the devil or the Word will have to bow. *And I guarantee it won't be the Word that bows!* If you stand firmly on the promises of God, the devil will have to bow and take his adversity with him.

A SHOCKING ATTITUDE

But the army of Israel forgot that. They allowed Goliath's appearance of strength to terrify them into forgetting their covenant. And so, when David arrived at the camp to bring his three brothers some provisions, he was shocked at what he saw. He was shocked at the attitude of the armies of God. He was amazed to see the army of God breaking ranks and running away in fear from one man.

And as he talked with [his brothers], **behold, there came up the champion, the Philistine of Gath, Goliath by name, out of the armies of the Philistines, and spake according to the same words: and David heard them. And all the men of Israel, when they saw the man, fled from him, and were sore afraid. And the men of**

Israel said, Have ye seen this man that is come up? surely to defy Israel is he come up: and it shall be, that the man who killeth him, the king will enrich him with great riches, and will give him his daughter, and make his father's house free in Israel. And David spake to the men that stood by him, saying, What shall be done to the man that killeth this Philistine, and taketh away the reproach from Israel? for who is this uncircumcised Philistine, that he should defy the armies of the living God?

1 Samuel 17:23-26

As I said earlier, the men of Israel were afraid of what they saw. The first thing they said to David was, "Have you seen this man?"

Most of us have said something similar at one time or another. Maybe we weren't facing a literal giant, but we had a giant of a problem. We were facing what looked like an impossible situation. And someone said, "Well, let's just stand on the Word." And what did we say? "Have you seen this?" Or "That's easy for you to say, you're not in my place."

What we're really saying is that what we see has convinced us that it is bigger than God. When you say, "Have you seen this impossible situation I'm faced with? If you knew what it was like to be facing what I'm facing, you wouldn't be talking so boldly," you're saying that what has robbed you of your boldness is bigger than God.

That's really what the men of Israel were thinking. In effect they were telling David that Goliath was bigger than the Most High God. Their wrong perspective caused them to be defeated.

But as we saw earlier, David had a different point of view. Where his brothers and the other men of Israel saw only opposition, adversity and an impossible situation, David saw opportunity for a great victory. David saw opportunity to excel, to reap a reward. David remembered his covenant. He remembered that there is nothing any of us can encounter that's bigger than God. God is the Most High God. And "Most High" is as high as you can get. There's nothing bigger than the Most High God.

"Have you seen this man?" David saw the same giant, the same man, that the men of the army of Israel saw. Goliath didn't get any smaller when David showed up. He wasn't less powerful when David saw him. He didn't have any less battle skill or any smaller weapons when David came to the camp. The problem David saw was the same one that had frightened the armies of Israel.

Too Big To Miss

But the difference between the men of Israel and David was in their perspectives. David saw the same thing the men of Israel saw, but his perspective was different. Consequently, he responded differently.

> **And David said to Saul, Let no man's heart fail because of him; thy servant will go and fight with this Philistine. And Saul said to David, Thou art not able to go against this Philistine to fight with him: for thou art but a youth, and he a man of war from his youth. And David said unto Saul, Thy servant kept his father's sheep, and there came a lion, and a bear, and took a lamb out of the flock: And I went out after him, and smote him, and**

delivered it out of his mouth: and when he arose against me, I caught him by his beard, and smote him, and slew him. Thy servant slew both the lion and the bear: and this uncircumcised Philistine shall be as one of them, seeing he hath defied the armies of the living God. David said moreover, The Lord that delivered me out of the paw of the lion, and out of the paw of the bear, he will deliver me out of the hand of this Philistine.

1 Samuel 17:32-37

David volunteered to fight the Philistine giant because his perspective was different than that of the other men of Israel. When they saw Goliath, they said, "He's too big to kill." But when David saw Goliath, he said, "He's too big to miss!" It was the same giant. One man was defeated because he said, "He's too big to kill." But another man was victorious because he said, "He's too big to miss."

It's all a matter of perspective, or point of view. Some people run and hide from the problem; others thrive on overcoming problems. Some people see only the adversaries blocking the way; others look beyond the adversaries to the opportunities behind them.

OBSTACLES OR GOALS?

When God presents you with an opportunity, the perspective you have on it has everything to do with whether you seize that opportunity. Someone once said, "Obstacles are what we see when we take our eyes off our goals." When all you see are obstacles, that's an indication that you're no longer focused on your goals or on your vision.

And when you're no longer focused on your God-given vision, you're no longer focused on Jesus. The Bible tells us to keep our eyes on Jesus.

> **Looking unto Jesus the author and finisher of our faith; who for the joy that was set before him endured the cross, despising the shame, and is set down at the right hand of the throne of God. For consider him that endured such contradiction of sinners against himself, lest ye be wearied and faint in your minds.**
>
> **Hebrews 12:2,3**

Jesus, the Word, has the answer to every problem. So if all you talk about is the problem, that is a sure indication that you don't have your eyes on the answer. The answer is in Jesus. If all you see are obstacles, then it is obvious that you have taken your eyes off of the goals.

A List of Excuses

Here is a list of six excuses that will keep you from seizing your God-given opportunities. Read these negative statements and make a point of removing them from your vocabulary.

1. "It's impossible."

2. "It can't be done."

3. "I don't have what it takes."

4. "It's too risky."

5. "What if it doesn't work?"

6. "What if I lose everything I have?"

THEN YOU START OVER

Let me elaborate on that sixth one for a moment—
"What if I lose everything I have?" The answer to that one
is "You start over."

Back in the early 1990s, Carolyn and I were faced with
the most severe financial crisis we had ever faced since
we'd been in full-time ministry. This crisis reached the
point that we had to make a decision to be willing to lose
everything and start over. For a while it looked as if we
would lose our buildings, our equipment, our staff, our
money, even our home. But were we going to lose our
ministry? No!

I won't lose my ministry just because I lose my buildings, my equipment, my staff, my money or my home. My
ministry can't be taken away from me, because my
ministry is in me. I'm not finished in the ministry just
because all of my earthly possessions are taken. My
ministry is in me. You can't take that from me *unless I'm
willing to give it up.*

So my ministry is not over if I lose my building.
"Where will you preach?" On the street.

It's not over if I lose my sound system. "How will they
hear you?" I'll preach louder.

"Well, if you lose your car, how will you get there?"
Hitchhike. Walk.

"If you have to lay off your staff, how will you get
everything done?" Work all night.

We had to get to the point that we were even willing
to sell our home—our dream home that we had designed
and built ourselves—and put all the money into the
ministry if that was what it took to keep us going.

God turned that situation around, and, fortunately, it didn't take that. We didn't have to do that. But we were willing to do it. We were willing to lose everything we had in the natural because we realized that losing all our possessions would not mean we'd lost our ministry. My ministry is inside me. It doesn't depend on worldly possessions.

Seizing God-given opportunities requires that you get rid of all negative excuses. Stop saying "It's too risky." "It's impossible." "I don't have what it takes—the money, equipment, time, support or whatever." "What if I lose everything?" You'll never seize an opportunity by hanging onto your security, or what you perceive to be security. The things that you and I tend to think are security, the Bible says are not security at all. I believe it was General Douglas MacArthur who said, "There is no such thing as security—only opportunity."

The Only Security

Now we know we have security in God. We know we have security in the Holy Spirit. But the temporal things we tend to think of as secure are not. We think, "Oh, my home is security." No, it isn't. Ask the people whose homes have been blown away by hurricanes or tornadoes. Your home can be here one day and gone the next. "Well, I've still got my business or my job or my car." How many businesses go broke overnight? How many employers are laying off workers? How many cars get repossessed or stolen or wrecked?

None of these things are secure. The only secure thing you and I have is the Word of God. All we have are opportunities—opportunities to use our faith.

Isaiah said, **The grass withereth, the flower fadeth: but the word of our God shall stand for ever** (40:8). If you're standing on the Word of God, you're beginning to build a secure base. You're building a solid foundation for your life. But all these other things we think are security are not secure. The Bible even says a man's life is but a vapor (James 4:14). The Word of God is the only security.

Attitude Dictates Performance

Attitude—the way we perceive things—is important because it determines our outcomes. For instance, the performance of an airplane depends upon its attitude. If you raise the nose of the airplane, you have changed its attitude and consequently, the performance of the airplane. If you lower the nose, you change the attitude and consequently, the performance.

It's the same in life. Your attitude dictates your performance. If you have a wrong attitude, you will perform poorly. Many Christians seem to have a negative attitude about everything. You say, "Good morning!" to them, and they say, "Just wait—all hell will break loose before lunch." I've known Christians who got upset over the expression, "Have a good day." Have you ever seen people who got mad at you when you told them to have a good day?

There were Christians who got mad at Oral Roberts for saying, "Something good is going to happen to you." Some religious people got mad at him for saying, "God is a good God." And when he said God wants you to prosper and be in health even as your soul prospers (3 John 2), they were really angry. They wanted to stay negative. They wanted to stay broke and sick and continue to be failures.

Some Christians become angry if you try to take away their tribulations. "Bless God, we've been tribulating for forty years, and you're not going to stop us. Do you understand?"

"Jesus said in the world we shall have tribulations, and we're scriptural. We're the First Church of the Tribulation."

Yes, Jesus did say we would have tribulation in the world, but that's not where He stopped. He said, **In the world ye shall have tribulation: but be of good cheer; I have overcome the world** (John 16:33).

WRONG IDENTIFICATION

You see, you can identify with the wrong thing. You can identify with the tribulation of the world, or you can identify with Jesus and His victory over the world.

The psalmist said, **Many are the afflictions of the righteous** (Psalm 34:19), and many people stop reading right there and identify with the afflictions. But that's not where the psalmist stopped. The complete verse says, **Many are the afflictions of the righteous: but the Lord delivereth him out of them all.** That's where our identification should be—with the deliverance, not with the afflictions.

Now, I'm not saying you won't experience afflictions, trials or tribulation in this life. You will. If you make a decision to live by faith, you will have trials. You will have tribulations. You will have adversity. But the point is that the Lord delivers us out of them all.

Most Christians need to raise the levels of their attitudes. We need to change the way we think. Your attitude, your perspective on things, can be your best friend or your worst enemy. Let's raise our attitudes up to a positive level and stop identifying with the negative things in life.

No Use Looking at Ashes

Several years ago, I was asked to preach at Lester Sumrall's church. When I arrived by plane, one of his sons picked me up at the airport. About the first thing he said to me was, "Did you hear about our television station burning down?"

I said, "Yes, as a matter of fact, I did hear about it. What did Brother Sumrall say when it happened?"

And he said, "He wasn't here when the fire occurred, but as soon as he got home and we picked him up at the airport, I said, 'Daddy, the television station burned down. Do you want to go see it?'"

But Brother Sumrall just shook his head. "No," he said, "why would I want to see the ashes? Build it back."

Now that's the proper perspective on adversity. That's a positive attitude. Brother Sumrall refused to go look at the ashes of his television station. He just looked at the opportunity to start over—and maybe build it better.

The Biggest Fire

Thomas Edison had a similar experience. His son used to tell the story that when Thomas Edison was working in his laboratory on some experiments that he couldn't get to come out right, he would work late into the night and often sleep in the lab. One night the lab caught on fire. Of course the place was full of chemicals and other materials that were highly flammable, and the whole building went up in a huge blaze.

Apparently, the fire was so big it could be seen for miles. Fire departments from several different communities came to try to put out the fire, but they couldn't stop it because there wasn't enough water pressure.

At first they couldn't find Mr. Edison, and they were getting really concerned about him. But then his son found him standing off to the side watching the fire. And the son said, "Daddy, are you all right?" And when Mr. Edison said, "I'm fine," the son said, "The laboratory is burning to the ground. What are we going to do?"

"Go get your mother," Mr. Edison said. "Tell her this is the biggest fire I've ever seen. Tell her we may not have an opportunity to see one this big again."

And the next day, after the fire was out, he started building a new laboratory. He must have been pretty confident to have that kind of attitude. He didn't look at the adversity, but only at the opportunity.

A Breakthrough Every Day

We need to raise the level of our attitudes. Stop saying, "If I could just get a break. I never succeed because I never get a break." Yes, you do. Breaks, short for "breakthroughs," come to you every day. God gives you opportunities every day. But if you're busy feeling sorry for yourself, you'll be insensitive to them. You won't recognize them.

You don't have to depend on someone else or on circumstances to give you a break. The Bible says, **A man's gift maketh room for him, and bringeth him before great men** (Proverbs 18:16). God is the God of the breakthrough. God is giving you potential breakthroughs every day of your life. All you have to do is seize them. The reason we don't take advantage of break-throughs is that we're insensitive to them.

Thomas Edison said, "There are many more opportunities than there are people who see them." New opportunities come every day. You should get up every morning rejoicing because that day could bring the opportunities you need to come up to the level of life God has intended for you.

MY *NEXT* MASTERPIECE

At the age of eighty-three, the great architect Frank Lloyd Wright was asked, "Which of all the beautiful structures you've designed and built do you consider your greatest masterpiece?" And he answered, "My next one."

Which is your greatest opportunity? Your next one. Every day, God brings you a new opportunity to serve Him in a greater capacity. But you have to seize those opportunities, and to seize them, you must have the right attitude. Your future will look bright if your attitude is right. What someone says is impossible can be someone else's opportunity for greatness.

BREAKING THE BARRIER

Let me give you an example of how your attitude can affect your performance.

For decades, track and field experts said that no one would ever run a mile in fewer than four minutes. In the minds of most sports experts, this was a barrier that could not be broken.

But a runner named Roger Bannister refused to believe it. And he broke that barrier. He became the first person to run a mile in fewer than four minutes.

And right behind him came other runners who broke the barrier. And now there are hundreds of athletes who can run a mile in fewer than four minutes. The four-minute mile barrier has been broken hundreds of times since Mr. Bannister first broke it.

Since it is obviously possible for a runner to run a mile in fewer than four minutes, why hadn't anyone done it before Mr. Bannister? They hadn't done it, because their thinking was wrong. The barrier was in their minds. All of the so-called "experts" said it couldn't be done, and the majority of track and field athletes followed the crowd and believed it was impossible. So they didn't try to break that barrier. They just accepted that it couldn't be done.

But Mr. Bannister didn't accept it. He didn't believe in the impossibility. So he kept practicing and developing himself. He kept believing he could break the barrier, and eventually he did it. And almost right on his heels, several other runners broke the barrier. Now it was no longer a barrier. You see, what one person says is impossible can be another person's opportunity for greatness.

When someone says, "You can't have a strong church in this city," you ought to think, "Aha! An opportunity for greatness. An opportunity for effectual service for the Lord."

When someone says, "You can't have revival in that nation," you ought to think, "That's a barrier that can be broken. God wants it broken. Why couldn't He use me to break it? Here I am, Lord. Send me—not so I'll be glorified but so You will be glorified."

FEAR OF FAILURE

If there are barriers in your life or in my life, they are there because we have created them. We have allowed them to be there because we have listened to someone who has said that what God has called us to do is impossible. And when we think that something is impossible, we don't try to do it. If we perceive something as a barrier, we won't try to go beyond it. We let fear of failure hold us back.

Have you ever failed? Be honest now. Have you failed more than once? If you haven't failed at least once, you might as well stop reading this book because I have nothing to say to you. But, of course, everyone has failed at least once. People whom you and I consider great achievers and very successful people have failed. But they became successful *because they recognized that failure is not final.*

Setbacks are not permanent. Setbacks are only temporary. How long they last is determined by how long you allow them to last in your thinking.

Have you ever read Kenneth Hagin's book *Right and Wrong Thinking*[1]? If you haven't, I recommend it, and if you have read it, it might be good for you to read it again. Basically, what Brother Hagin says in that book is that we get negative results because we think improperly. We have a wrong attitude, and that wrong attitude affects our performance and our outcomes.

The truth is that barriers can be broken. Obstacles can be overcome. Mountains can be removed and cast into the sea. Impossibilities can become possibilities.

We must not allow ourselves to become stagnant and inoperative because of the fear of failure.

---

[1] Hagin, Kenneth E. *Right and Wrong Thinking*. Tulsa: Faith Library Publications, 1984.

Not Until You Say It

You are not a failure until you say you are. You're not a failure because you lost your home or your car. You're not a failure because your marriage ended in divorce, or because you have no relationship with your children, or because you got laid off at work.

You're not a failure because someone else says you are. You're only a failure when *you say you are.* You're only a failure when you accept failure. *To accept failure as final in your life is to finally become a failure.*

A Lion in the Street

Fear of failure is related to slothfulness. We've said all along that many people don't seize their opportunities, because they're unwilling to work hard.

Proverbs 22:13 says, **The slothful man saith, There is a lion without, I shall be slain in the streets.** I've always thought this verse is one of the funniest verses in the Bible. The man described here is trapped in negative thinking. He thinks that just because someone said there is a lion loose in the streets, he will be killed. That's like saying when you are in your car, "There is an eighteen-wheeler on the interstate. We shall all be killed." If you believed that, you would never leave home.

Just because there's a lion loose does not mean you're going to be slain. After all, there are a number of things you could do to avoid being slain. You could run. You could hide. You could call 9-1-1. But the slothful man is paralyzed by the fear of what he thinks might happen, and so he does nothing. He is a failure because he has accepted failure.

A GRASSHOPPER MENTALITY

Negative thinking and a wrong perspective can give you what we might call a "grasshopper" mentality. I'm sure you're familiar with the story in the book of Numbers about the twelve spies Moses sent out on a reconnaissance mission to the Promised Land. Even though they saw that it was a land flowing with milk and honey, ten of the twelve gave an evil report of the land when they came back. Joshua and Caleb told Moses they should immediately take possession of the land, but the other ten spies said,

> **We be not able to go up against the people; for they are stronger than we. And they brought up an evil report of the land which they had searched unto the children of Israel, saying, The land, through which we have gone to search it, is a land that eateth up the inhabitants thereof; and all the people that we saw in it are men of a great stature. And there we saw the giants, the sons of Anak, which come of the giants: and we were in our own sight as grasshoppers, and so we were in their sight.**

> **Numbers 13:31-33**

Just like the men of the army of Israel when they saw Goliath, these men saw what looked liked giants in the land they had gone to spy out, and they became afraid of them. They said, in effect, "These men are so much bigger than we are that we're only grasshoppers in comparison." They saw themselves as grasshoppers. Because of their fear, they decided that their adversaries were too big to overcome.

But their negative thinking didn't stop there. Their wrong perspective didn't stop with seeing themselves as grasshoppers. They thought the men of the Promised Land also saw them as grasshoppers.

But how did they know? They never got close enough to the giants to ask them. They didn't know what the giants thought. They never went up to them and asked, "How do you perceive us? Do we look like grasshoppers to you?" They were afraid to go anywhere near them. When they accepted that grasshopper mentality, they believed that was how everyone else saw them too.

We may think we look like grasshoppers, but that's not what we look like to God. To God we look like overcomers.

God didn't create us to be failures, and He doesn't give us opportunities to serve Him and to go up and take possession of our promised land without giving us the supernatural ability to do it. As we'll find out in the next chapter, God created us to be successful. We are designed by God to be winners.

CHAPTER 6

❖ ❖ ❖

CREATED TO BE A SUCCESS

God designed us to be successful. We can seize our God-given opportunities and turn them into realities *because we were created and designed by God to be successful in every endeavor in our lives.*

We don't have to be failures. We're not designed by God to fail. We are designed by God to win. I know some people have the philosophy that "it's not whether you win or lose, it's how you play the game that counts." Well, I didn't like that when my baseball coach said it to me when I was nine years old, and I don't like it now. I found out that if you play baseball right, you win.

Every time we played the game right, every time we played better than the opposing team, we won! Winning was the purpose of playing the game.

Winning is God's purpose for our lives. And I can prove that to you from the Bible.

FROM THE VERY BEGINNING

God's intention to create winners is obvious from the very first chapter of the Bible. In Genesis 1:26, God said, **Let us make man in our image.** Now let me pause right there for a moment.

Have you ever known God to fail? No, of course not. God is not a failure. It would be totally against the nature of God to fail, wouldn't it? And we are made in God's image. We are created in the image of the God who resides within us in the person of the Holy Spirit. Therefore, we were not designed to fail. God has designed us to be winners in every area of our lives.

And God said, Let us make man in our image, after our likeness: and let them have dominion over the fish of the sea, and over the fowl of the air, and over the cattle, and over all the earth, and over every creeping thing that creepeth upon the earth. So God created man in his own image, in the image of God created he him; male and female created he them. And God blessed them, and God said unto them, Be fruitful, and multiply, and replenish the earth, and subdue it: and have dominion over the fish of the sea, and over the fowl of the air, and over every living thing that moveth upon the earth.

Genesis 1:26-28

Notice that the first thing God did after creating the man and the woman was to bless them. When God blesses people, He empowers them to prosper. So we see that from the very beginning, God's intent was for man to prosper and be successful.

When God said to Adam and Eve, "Be blessed," He "conferred well-being or prosperity"[1] on them. Immediately after creating them, He empowered them to prosper.

---

[1] *The American Heritage Dictionary of the English Language,* (New York, Houghton Mifflin, 1970), p. 141.

He obviously wanted them to be successful in all that they did. I don't think it's any different today. God has not changed His mind. It was God's original intention for man to prosper, and it's still His intention for us today.

BE FRUITFUL

Right after He blessed them, God said to the man and woman, **Be fruitful** (Genesis 1:28). Now I want you to take particular note of the word *fruitful* because we're going to find that word a number of times in the Scriptures we will study in this chapter. It might be a good idea for you to underline or highlight that word in your Bible.

> **And God blessed them, and God said unto them, Be fruitful, and multiply, and replenish the earth, and subdue it: and have dominion over the fish of the sea, and over the fowl of the air, and over every living thing that moveth upon the earth.**
>
> **Genesis 1:28**

Again we see God's plan. God's plan from the beginning was that man be empowered to prosper and that man be fruitful. Of course, being fruitful can involve a number of things, but what I want to look at in this chapter is the relationship of fruitfulness to success. I'm saying here that to be fruitful is to be successful. The Bible tells us that from the beginning God empowered man to prosper and *commanded* him to be fruitful.

Now, if God expressed His desire for me to prosper and be fruitful as a command, that ought to answer these questions: *Is it God's will for me to prosper? Is it God's will for me to be successful? Is it God's will for every one of my endeavors to bear fruit?* If God commanded me to be fruitful, I would be out of the will of God if I didn't produce fruit, wouldn't I?

Being fruitful was God's will for Adam, His first man. And Jesus, the second Adam, came to restore the plan of God for man. Satan distracted the first Adam and caused a detour in God's perfect plan for man to prosper and to be fruitful, but Jesus came to restore God's original plan for our lives.

Therefore, I believe God is saying to you and to me today, "I empower you to prosper, and I command you to be successful."

A FRESH START

Now before you start scratching your head and saying, "Aw, come on, Brother Jerry, that sounds a little far-fetched," let's look at some more instances in the book of Genesis where God blessed people and commanded them to be fruitful.

The next example is in Genesis 9:1. Of course quite a few things had happened in the centuries since God had blessed Adam in the first chapter of Genesis. We know that man committed high treason against God and was exiled from the Garden of Eden. We know that as a result of sin, the imaginations of men became evil continually. We know that God regretted that He had created man and, therefore, had sent a flood to destroy all life on earth except Noah and his family and the animals God instructed him to bring into the ark.

But what did God do immediately after the flood waters had receded and Noah and his family had come out of the ark?

And God blessed Noah and his sons, and said unto them, Be fruitful, and multiply, and replenish the earth.

Genesis 9:1

Noah represents a fresh start, a new beginning after the fall of man. And the very first thing God did was to bless Noah. The very first thing He did for Noah was the same thing He had done for Adam. He blessed him. He empowered Noah and his sons to prosper. And He said to them, **Be fruitful, and multiply, and replenish the earth.**

Do you see what was happening? It was now hundreds of years later since the creation of Adam, but the command of God had not changed even though sin had entered the earth. Man had fallen, and Satan had become, so to speak, the illegitimate stepfather of mankind. But the plan of God had not changed. God was still blessing man and empowering him to prosper, and He was still commanding man to be fruitful and to be successful.

EXCEEDINGLY FRUITFUL

This theme of God's blessing and His command to be fruitful continues with the story of Abram. When God told Abram to leave his country and go to the land of Canaan, God conferred blessing on Abram. He empowered Abram to prosper, and He promised to bless everyone who blessed Abram. Then when Abram was ninety-nine years old, God promised to make him fruitful.

And when Abram was ninety years old and nine, the Lord appeared to Abram, and said unto him, I am the Almighty God; walk before me, and be thou perfect. And I will

make my covenant between me and thee, and will multiply thee exceedingly. And Abram fell on his face: and God talked with him, saying, As for me, behold, my covenant is with thee, and thou shalt be a father of many nations. Neither shall thy name any more be called Abram, but thy name shall be Abraham; for a father of many nations have I made thee. And I will make thee exceeding fruitful, and I will make nations of thee, and kings shall come out of thee.

Genesis 17:1-6

Again we see the same pattern. God empowered Adam to prosper. He empowered Noah to prosper. He empowered Abraham to prosper. And along with each blessing, each empowerment, God gave the command to be fruitful.

Dig Another Well

God's plan didn't stop with Adam, Noah and Abraham. In Genesis 26 we see God empowering Abraham's son, Isaac, to prosper and be fruitful even in adversity.

And there was a famine in the land, beside the first famine that was in the days of Abraham. And Isaac went unto Abimelech king of the Philistines unto Gerar. And the Lord appeared unto him, and said, Go not down into Egypt; dwell in the land which I shall tell thee of: Sojourn in this land, and I will be with thee, and will bless thee; for unto thee, and unto thy seed, I will give all these countries, and I will perform the oath which I sware unto Abraham thy father; And I will make thy seed to multiply as the stars of heaven, and will give unto thy seed all these countries; and in thy seed shall all the nations of the earth be blessed....

Then Isaac sowed in that land, and received in the same year an hundredfold: and the Lord blessed him. And the man waxed great, and went forward, and grew until he became very great: For he had possession of flocks, and possession of herds, and great store of servants: and the Philistines envied him....

And Isaac digged again the wells of water, which they had digged in the days of Abraham his father; for the Philistines had stopped them after the death of Abraham: and he called their names after the names by which his father had called them. And Isaac's servants digged in the valley, and found there a well of springing water. And the herdmen of Gerar did strive with Isaac's herdmen, saying, The water is ours: and he called the name of the well Esek; because they strove with him. And they digged another well, and strove for that also: and he called the name of it Sitnah. And he removed from thence, and digged another well; and for that they strove not: and he called the name of it Rehoboth; and he said, For now

the Lord hath made room for us, and we shall be fruitful in the land.

Genesis 26:1-4,12-14,18-22

Are you paying close attention to the word *fruitful* in each of these passages? The story of Isaac demonstrates that God's blessing and fruitfulness are not dependent on circumstances. God empowered Isaac to prosper, and he did, even though there was a famine in the land and many adversaries were against him.

FRUITFUL IN THE LAND OF AFFLICTION

Joseph also was a man who was blessed and fruitful even in a situation where, in the natural, there was no possibility of bearing fruit. When his sons were born, Joseph gave them names that reminded him of God's blessing in the midst of adversity.

And Joseph called the name of the first-born Manasseh: For God, said he, hath made me forget all my toil, and all my father's house. And the name of the second called he Ephraim: For God hath caused me to be fruitful in the land of my affliction.

Genesis 41:51,52

Joseph declared that God had made him fruitful even in the land where in the natural it would have been impossible for him to be fruitful. He understood that it makes no difference what kind of opposition you may experience. It makes no difference what kind of adversity there is. It makes no difference where you live. God can cause you to be prosperous and fruitful in the land of your affliction.

No matter where you are or what's going on in the natural, the command of God is on your life to be fruitful.

Both Isaac and Joseph were in places where success looked impossible. Isaac was among enemies during a severe drought. Joseph had been sold into slavery and was in prison in Egypt. But God gave each of them opportunities to prosper, and because they seized those opportunities, they were able to fulfill God's command to be fruitful.

THE PLAN HASN'T CHANGED

"Wait a minute," you may be thinking, "all these examples are from the Old Testament. What about the New Testament?"

All right, let's go to the New Testament, and I'll show you that God's plan for us to succeed and bear fruit hasn't changed.

In his letter to the church at Colossae, the apostle Paul prayed this prayer:

> **For this cause we also, since the day we heard it, do not cease to pray for you, and to desire that ye might be filled with the knowledge of his will in all wisdom and spiritual understanding; That ye might walk worthy of the Lord unto all pleasing, being fruitful in every good work, and increasing in the knowledge of God.**
>
> **Colossians 1:9,10**

Notice the phrase **that ye might walk worthy of the Lord unto all pleasing, being fruitful in every good work.** I think we could paraphrase that as "being fruitful or successful in every endeavor."

The Amplified Bible says, **That you may walk (live and conduct yourselves) in a manner worthy of the Lord, fully pleasing to Him and desiring to please Him in all things, bearing fruit in every good work and steadily growing and increasing in and by the knowledge of God [with fuller, deeper, and clearer insight, acquaintance, and recognition]** (Colossians 1:10).

Once again, take note of the phrase **bearing fruit in every good work.** God is saying here by the Holy Ghost to New Testament believers, "My plan has not changed for man. My will has not changed. I commanded Adam to be blessed and to be fruitful. And I still want My people to be fruitful, or successful, in every endeavor."

We were created by God to be successful. He created us to seize the opportunities He presents us and bring them to reality. God is looking for a people in these last days who will not settle for anything less than success in every endeavor.

The Vine and the Branches

Jesus went into the subject of fruit bearing in depth in John 15:

I am the true vine, and my Father is the husbandman. Every branch in me that beareth not fruit he taketh away: and every branch that beareth fruit, he purgeth it, that it may bring forth more fruit. Now ye are clean through the word which I have spoken unto you. Abide in me, and I in you. As the branch cannot bear fruit of itself, except it abide in the vine; no more can ye, except ye abide in

me. I am the vine, ye are the branches: He that abideth in me, and I in him, the same bringeth forth much fruit: for without me ye can do nothing. If a man abide not in me, he is cast forth as a branch, and is withered; and men gather them, and cast them into the fire, and they are burned. If ye abide in me, and my words abide in you, ye shall ask what ye will, and it shall be done unto you. Herein is my Father glorified, that ye bear much fruit; so shall ye be my disciples.

John 15:1-8

I want you to underline the phrase **more fruit** in the second verse. Notice that God wants you to continually bear fruit. Bearing fruit is not a one-time event to God.

Now what the phrase **Herein is my Father glorified** reveals to me is that the more fruit I bear, the more glorified God becomes. And the statement **that ye bear much fruit; so shall ye be my disciples** suggests that one of the earmarks of a true disciple is that he or she bears much fruit.

The Amplified Bible makes even clearer God's attitude toward fruitfulness.

I am the True Vine, and My Father is the Vinedresser. Any branch in Me that does not bear fruit [that stops bearing] He cuts away (trims off, takes away); and He cleanses and repeatedly prunes every branch that continues to bear fruit, to make it bear more and richer and more excellent fruit.

John 15:1,2

It is obvious from these verses that God not only wants us to be fruitful, but He, as the Vinedresser, will do what is necessary to point out to us what we need to strip away, remove or prune so we can bear more fruit. In other words, even though I may have achieved a certain level of success in my life up to now, if I'm going to be more successful in the future, I have to get ready for more pruning.

I know we don't enjoy hearing that. But the truth is that I can't be any more successful than I am right now until I experience some more pruning. Of course, pruning is not always comfortable because pruning means to cut off, cut out or strip away something that is attached to me or that I am attached to.

However, if I'm to reach the next level of success, I have to submit to God's pruning. The Word says that any branch in Him that is bearing fruit He prunes repeatedly so that it can bear more fruit. So I can't question pruning or back away from it, because God's pruning causes me to reach the next level of success.

"It's Pruning Time"

The apostle Paul said it this way: **All things are lawful unto me, but all things are not expedient** (1 Corinthians 6:12). He was saying that he had discovered things in his life which were not necessarily sinful, but were no longer expedient, or profitable. And he realized God was saying to him, "It's pruning time."

There may be things right now in your life that are not necessarily sinful, but are no longer profitable. They may have even become distractions. They may be holding you back from reaching the higher level of success and fruitfulness God has for you.

The way to prune is to cut or strip away. That doesn't sound comfortable, does it? Suppose I went out and said to my pear tree, "Pear tree, it's pruning time. We want you to bear more fruit." I'm quite sure that if the pear tree could talk, it would say, "Please do not put that saw to my limbs. That hurts!"

And it may seem strange that we prune the tree even though it was loaded with pears last season. But if we don't prune it, we will have seen all of the fruit ever seen on that pear tree. That tree will have reached its highest level of success if it's not pruned.

It's the same way with us. Now, don't throw the book down and walk off saying, "I don't need pruning." We all need pruning.

I've learned to welcome pruning. I want God to reveal to me what needs to be stripped away, cut off and cut out, because I have not yet attained the level of success I know God has in store for me. But I'm pursuing it. I want it not only so I can bring a greater blessing to humanity, but also so I can bring more glory to my heavenly Father.

And I believe your reading this book is evidence that you want the same thing.

ABIDE IN HIM

Jesus said in John 15 that we were created by God to be fruitful. But the secret to bearing much fruit is to be totally dependent upon Him. We must abide continually in Him if we are to bear fruit.

Dwell in Me, and I will dwell in you. [Live in Me, and I will live in you.] Just as no branch can bear fruit of itself without

> abiding in (being vitally united to) the vine, neither can you bear fruit unless you abide in Me. I am the Vine; you are the branches. Whoever lives in Me and I in him bears much (abundant) fruit. However, apart from Me [cut off from vital union with Me] you can do nothing.
>
> John 15:4,5 AMP

Our fruitfulness, our success, is directly linked to our union with Christ. Outside of Him, we are limited. But when we are vitally united to Him, our potential for success is unlimited. Why? Because He is the source.

Jesus is the source because He is the Vine. When you are linked up with the Vine, you have a partner in life. You have a partner in life who is rich, who has unlimited resources, who has never failed at any endeavor. When you abide in Jesus, you have a partner in life who will never fail.

When you're linked to the Vine, when you're linked to Jesus, you have a partner in life who is totally unlimited. And when you fully realize that you are linked up with the Creator of the universe, you become confident that you have at your disposal the same power the Creator used to create the world.

The same power God used to create the universe is available to you and me. We're fully equipped to be whatever God has called us to be. We're fully equipped to have whatever God says we can have. And we're fully equipped to do whatever God says we can do.

Our Responsibility

We need to be continually pruned because it's the "dead wood" in our lives that keeps us from reaching our full potential. Just as dead wood must be pruned from a fruit tree, we must prune the dead wood out of our lives so we can bear more fruit.

What do I mean by dead wood in our lives? *The Amplified Bible* calls it every **encumbrance (unnecessary weight) and that sin which so readily (deftly and cleverly) clings to and entangles us...** (Hebrews 12:1 AMP).

The writer of Hebrews goes on to say, **Let us run with patient endurance and steady and active persistence the appointed course of the race that is set before us. Looking away [from all that will distract] to Jesus, Who is the Leader and the Source of our faith...** (Hebrews 12:1,2 AMP).

"Dead wood" is anything that encumbers us, distracts us from following Jesus single-mindedly or becomes an unnecessary weight. These are the things that God wants pruned out of our lives. The most productive people in the kingdom of God are people who are constantly being pruned. They are people who are constantly stripping the dead wood away and removing distractions.

But it isn't God Himself who does the pruning. Second Timothy 2:21 says, **If a man therefore purge himself...he shall be a vessel unto honour, sanctified, and meet for the master's use, and prepared unto every good work.** God will point out what needs to be purged or pruned, but it's our responsibility to do the purging or pruning. God won't do that for us. He will point out the dead wood, but we must be obedient to strip it out of our lives ourselves.

Pruning brings us to the place of conformity to the will of God. When I allow myself to be pruned, I bring myself into conformity with God's will. And therefore, I am enabled to become more and more fruitful. If we're going to do God's will, we must get rid of everything that is no longer profitable or that has become a distraction. I don't know what it might be for you, but let me give you an example from my own life.

CROSSING THE LINE

When I get into something, I really get into it. I don't know any boundaries. For instance, when I get into ministry, I get into it all the way. If God says "Go ye," I don't know when to "stop ye"! Do you understand what I'm saying? I'm deeply dedicated and deeply committed to what I'm called to do, and I don't know when or where to stop.

Now, being deeply committed to ministry is fine, but because of this tendency in my nature, I have to watch myself in other areas and other activities. I have to watch myself because it's my nature to go all out in anything that I do. And there are some things I enjoy as hobbies or as recreation, but I have to be very careful that I don't allow these activities to consume me. I have to be careful that I don't cross the line between enjoying a little time out for recreation and allowing a hobby to consume time I should be giving to God.

I always know when I've crossed that line. God doesn't have to tell me. I always know when I've allowed myself to indulge in something too much and it's taking away from time with God.

One of the activities I enjoy most is riding motorcycles. I've been riding motorcycles as long as I can remember, and I enjoy them. A few years ago, I was blessed with a brand new Harley Davidson motorcycle that had everything on it but an air conditioner and a microwave oven!

It was the most gorgeous motorcycle I'd ever owned. I loved it. But one day when I was riding it out near my ministry headquarters, I knew I had crossed the line.

Now, it's not a sin for me to own a motorcycle. But at that particular time it was no longer profitable. It was lawful, but it wasn't expedient, because it was consuming too much of my time. It had gotten to the point that I wanted to spend all of my time in a motorcycle shop. I had to have all of the magazines, clothes, accessories. I'd gotten completely into it. I thought, "Well, I can't ride a motorcycle in just jeans and a T-shirt and tennis shoes. I've got to have all the right stuff." I had so many accessories for that motorcycle that my garage began to look like a Harley Davidson dealership.

My friends started teasing me and calling me the "accessory king." One of them said, "Jerry, is your underwear Harley Davidson too?" I said, "You know, I hadn't thought of that." I didn't have any Harley Davidson underwear, but believe me, I had every other Harley Davidson accessory. And suddenly, I knew I'd crossed the line. God didn't have to tell me. Nobody else had to tell me. I knew.

And riding that motorcycle home one day, suddenly I realized I was riding someone else's motorcycle. It wasn't mine anymore.

TOY OR TOOL?

So right there, deliberately, all by myself without any prompting from God, I said, "Lord, to me this motorcycle is a toy. But there's somebody out there to whom this can become a tool. And I want to turn my toy into a tool. So I want You to reveal to me the person You want me to give this to."

And I said, "I'm doing this to show You first of all that You are the most important thing in my life. Not a Harley Davidson. And secondly, I want to show the devil that this motorcycle is not an idol to me. I'm doing it to show the devil he doesn't have any control in my life."

Well, immediately the devil spoke up and said, "Do you know how much this thing cost? And you're going to *give* it away. Why don't you sell it?" But I knew I'd put more pressure on him by giving it away than by selling it.

Now, there wouldn't have been anything wrong with selling it. But I wanted to put pressure on the devil and show him that, not only in word but in deed also, God has first place in my life. So I prayed, and I gave it to the person God directed me to give it to.

And for the next year I didn't get on another motorcycle. I didn't go near a motorcycle shop. I didn't pick up a motorcycle magazine. In fact, when some friends offered to lend me a bike so I could go with them on a motorcycle trip, I said, "Thanks, but I can't get involved in motorcycle activities right now. I'm not saying I'll never get on another motorcycle, but I can't do it right now."

Now God didn't make me give up motorcycles. I did this of my own free will. But I am convinced that God took notice. About two years later, He started giving me motorcycles again. In fact, He gave me two motorcycles, one for cruising and one for touring. I still have them, but my attitude toward them is totally different.

I ride them occasionally, and I still enjoy them; but I'm not consumed by them. I can ride them when I have time, enjoy the recreation, then put them away and go on about my business. God gave me an opportunity to prune myself, to strip away something that was holding me back from more effectual service to Him—and I seized that opportunity and achieved a higher level of success. Praise the Lord!

CHAPTER 7

◆ ◆ ◆

HOW TO RECEIVE GOD IDEAS

Throughout this book, we've been saying that every day God presents each of us with opportunities to serve Him in a greater capacity. In his first letter to the Corinthians, the apostle Paul said he could not come to visit them yet because he had been given an opportunity for more effectual service in Ephesus.

For a great door and effectual is opened unto me, and there are many adversaries.

1 Corinthians 16:9

Paul seized his opportunity because, as we've said, he recognized it, and he was willing to do whatever it took to lay hold of his God-given vision, suddenly and by force. He was willing to work hard, persevere, fight the good fight of faith against adversaries, prune off every weight and distraction that was holding him back and do whatever he had to do in order to bring his God-given opportunity into reality.

Paul was ready to seize every opportunity to serve God in a greater capacity and to rise to a higher level of faith and a deeper knowledge of God. He said that knowing God in Jesus Christ was his highest goal, one for which he was ready to lose everything else to attain.

But what things were gain to me, those I counted loss for Christ. Yea doubtless, and I count all things but loss for the excellency of the knowledge of Christ Jesus my Lord: for whom I have suffered the loss of all things, and do count them but dung, that I may win Christ, And be found in him, not having mine own righteousness, which is of the law, but that which is through the faith of Christ, the righteousness which is of God by faith: That I may know him, and the power of his resurrection, and the fellowship of his sufferings, being made conformable unto his death; If by any means I might attain unto the resurrection of the dead. Not as though I had already attained, either were already perfect: but I follow after, if that I may apprehend that for which also I am apprehended of Christ Jesus. Brethren, I count not myself to have apprehended: but this one thing I do, forgetting those things which are behind, and reaching forth unto those things which are before, I press toward the mark for the prize of the high calling of God in Christ Jesus.

Philippians 3:7-14

Here Paul gives us another key to seizing God-given opportunities and achieving a higher level of success in our lives of faith. He was *hungry for God. His ultimate goal was to know the deep things of God, and he was willing to lose everything he had gained in the world to press forward continually toward that goal.*

A LIFELONG SEARCH

Hunger for God and a deeper revelation of His Word are the keys to receiving God-given opportunities and "God ideas." God ideas are ideas that come to us only through the wisdom of God, through His Word and through His Spirit speaking to our spirits.

God ideas cannot be found by searching for them with your natural wisdom. The Bible says,

> **Canst thou by searching find out God? canst thou find out the Almighty unto perfection? It is as high as heaven....**
>
> **Job 11:7,8**

God's thoughts are so much higher than our thoughts (Isaiah 55:8) that we cannot comprehend them except through God's revelation of them in our spirits. If we are going to receive God ideas, we must be spiritually hungry for them and search for them in God's Word.

Every Scripture is impregnated with the wisdom of God. Just about the time you've studied a Scripture until you're sure you've gotten it fixed in your spirit, you'll find that God has more revelation to give you from that particular Scripture. The more time you spend with God in His Word, the more He will reveal to you. His wisdom is inexhaustible. If you are willing to reach out for it in faith, you will never stop receiving revelation knowledge from every verse in the Bible.

But when you begin a quest for the deep things of God, the knowledge of God, you are starting a search that will last a lifetime. **Press**[ing] **toward the mark of the high calling of God in Christ Jesus** (Philippians 3:14) is a lifelong quest. It's an unending search. No one has ever discovered all there is to know about God. No matter how much you know, there's still plenty more God is eager to reveal to you.

How Much Can You Eat?

God ideas and God-given opportunities come to you in direct proportion to your hunger for them. How much of the deep things of God can your spirit conceive? How much can you take in?

More importantly, how much are you *willing* to take in? Old Testament believers like Job were limited in how much spiritual wisdom they could receive because they did not have the Holy Spirit abiding within them. But we don't have that problem. Our spiritual capacity is not limited. We are "in Christ" people. Through His Spirit residing in our spirits, we can receive as much of the deep things of God as we are willing to open ourselves up to.

It's been my experience that the more I receive revelation from God, the more spiritually hungry I become. I know a lot more about God than I did in 1969, when I first got a little bit of revelation about living by faith; *but I'm more hungry for God now than I was then.* The more spiritual food I eat, the more I want.

Indwelling Wisdom

Paul told the Colossians they could be rich in wisdom if they would only open themselves to the Word.

Let the word of Christ dwell in you richly in all wisdom; teaching and admonishing one another in psalms and hymns

**and spiritual songs, singing with grace in
your hearts to the Lord.**

Colossians 3:16

Now if the apostle Paul admonishes me to allow the
Word to dwell in me *richly,* that must mean that my capacity to receive the Word and God's wisdom is unlimited.
Remember from the last chapter that when we abide in
Christ we are hooked up with a partner who has unlimited
resources. Abiding in Christ removes the limitation on
how much of God we can grasp with our spirits.

The book of Acts says the Word of God is able to build
us up (Acts 20:32). That means it can charge you up the
way a generator charges a battery. When I study the Word,
I am hooked up to a dynamo called the Holy Ghost. You
can't stay depressed when you approach the Bible as the
richness of God's Word. You begin to look at it from a
different perspective. Do you remember how important
we said a change of perspective, or attitude, is to your
performance? When you no longer read the Bible with a
religious mind-set, you begin to expect it to explode in
your spirit every time you open it.

I realize that there are Christians who don't view Bible
reading that way. Reading and studying the Word has
become irksome to them. It has become a religious chore.
But these are not true Word people. These people don't
receive God ideas, because they are not hungry for the
Word. True Word people can't get enough of the Word of
God. To them, God's Word is rich. It's precious. It's price-
less. The more they get of it, the more they want.

DON'T STOP THERE!

As New Testament believers, we must be careful not
to limit ourselves to the perspective of the Old Testament

saints. We must remember that they couldn't have understood what you and I have access to in the things of God. And therefore, when we find a quotation from the Old Testament in the New Testament, we must be sure we go beyond the limitations of the old covenant.

First Corinthians 2:9 is a good example.

As it is written, Eye hath not seen, nor ear heard, neither have entered into the heart of man, the things which God hath prepared for them that love him.

Now if you stop reading right there, you have merely read a quotation from the Old Testament. Paul is quoting a verse from the prophet Isaiah (64:4). If you stop reading there, you might get the impression that you cannot receive the wisdom of God.

However, notice that the next verse starts with the conjunction *but.* That means Paul is not finished. It means he is about to make a contrast between what the Old Testament believers could receive and what we, as New Testament believers, can receive.

But, Paul says, **God hath revealed them unto us by his Spirit...** (1 Corinthians 2:10). "Us" means those of us who are "in Christ." Under the old covenant there were limitations. Their (spiritual) eyes couldn't see. Their (spiritual) ears couldn't hear. Their hearts couldn't conceive all that God had in store.

But we have received a better covenant. And under it, we have been filled with the Holy Ghost. Therefore, thank God, our eyes can see, our ears can hear and our hearts can conceive everything that God has prepared for those that love Him.

The remainder of verse 10 says, **for the Spirit searcheth all things, yea, the deep things of God.** One of the jobs of the Holy Ghost is to search the deep things of God and reveal them to us.

The Amplified Bible expands that verse to read,

> **Yet to us God has unveiled and revealed them by and through His Spirit, for the [Holy] Spirit searches diligently, exploring and examining everything, even sounding the profound and bottomless things of God [the divine counsels and things hidden and beyond man's scrutiny].**
>
> **1 Corinthians 2:10**

The Holy Ghost is searching diligently for the deep things of God that are beyond man's scrutiny. And He reveals them to "in Christ" people. He reveals them to believers like you and me.

THE MIND OF CHRIST

Paul says specifically that we have received the Spirit of God and can therefore know the things of the Spirit.

> **Now we have received, not the spirit of the world, but the spirit which is of God; that we might know the things that are freely given to us of God. Which things also we speak, not in the words which man's wisdom teacheth, but which the Holy Ghost teacheth; comparing spiritual things with spiritual. But the natural man receiveth not the things of the Spirit of God: for they are foolishness unto him: neither can he know them, because they**

are spiritually discerned. But he that is spiritual judgeth all things, yet he himself is judged of no man. For who hath known the mind of the Lord, that he may instruct him? But we have the mind of Christ.

1 Corinthians 2:12-16

Folks, we have spent too much time operating in our own mental capacities when we have within us the ability to operate in the mind of Christ. We have spent too long operating in our natural limitations instead of operating in the divine favor and blessing the Bible says have been [so freely and lavishly] bestowed on us by God (1 Corinthians 2:12 AMP).

DISASTROUS RESULTS

If we have within us the ability to operate in the mind of Christ, why don't we do it? Of course, there are a number of reasons, some of which we've already talked about in this book—laziness, fear of failure, insensitivity to the Spirit, cowardice in the face of adversaries, wrong perspective. But our failure to seize the opportunities God gives us to stretch ourselves to receive more of His wisdom has disastrous results.

Paul pointed out one of those results to the Christians at Corinth. He said he could not share with them all that Jesus had revealed to him, because they were still living too much in the flesh. They were still spiritual babies. Their refusal to grow up spiritually meant that he had to feed them "baby food" from the Word instead of the "meat" of the mysteries of God that the Holy Spirit wanted them to receive.

> And I, brethren, could not speak unto you as unto spiritual, but as unto carnal, even as unto babes in Christ. I have fed you with milk, and not with meat: for hitherto ye were not able to bear it, neither yet now are ye able. For ye are yet carnal: for whereas there is among you envying, and strife, and divisions, are ye not carnal, and walk as men?
>
> **1 Corinthians 3:1-3**

Paul had already told the Corinthians that he spoke to them **the wisdom of God in a mystery, even the hidden wisdom, which God ordained before the world unto our glory** (1 Corinthians 2:7), but they were having trouble receiving it because they were limiting themselves by living in the flesh instead of in the spirit.

Of course, Jesus had said to His disciples, **I have yet many things to say unto you, but ye cannot bear them now** (John 16:12). However, He said this before the Holy Ghost had been given to them, and so there were things that they weren't yet able to receive.

However, Paul says we *should* receive the deep mysteries of God. He prayed that we would be filled with the spirit of wisdom (Ephesians 1:17). Paul prayed that you and I would have access to the same knowledge Jesus had revealed to him. He prayed we would have the same ability to see into the deep things of God so that we might know the mysteries of God. But we won't receive insight into the mysteries of God if we refuse to grow past the point of eating spiritual baby food.

They Put on the Brakes

A number of years ago I was preaching in a meeting with Kenneth Copeland. We were both dealing with the laws of prosperity. When Brother Copeland began his message in the first service, I thought I knew exactly where he was going with it because he and I had sort of "preached" to each other about these things before the meeting had started. But I noticed he didn't go as deeply into the subject in the meeting as he and I had gone in our discussions.

It seemed he got right up to a certain point in his teaching on the laws of prosperity, and he couldn't go any further. "Well," I thought, "he's just laying a foundation here. He'll get to the revelation we discussed in the next service."

But he didn't. He came at the subject from a different angle, but when he got to that same point, he couldn't seem to go any further. And this happened every time he preached in that meeting.

Afterwards, I asked him, "Why didn't you get into what you and I talked about before this meeting?"

He said, "I couldn't. I did my best to get past that point, but the people couldn't receive it."

They couldn't receive it. Isn't that sad? It was a great meeting. People were blessed in many areas. But I walked away thinking, *If they only knew what they missed.* They put the brakes on. They limited themselves, and they limited God because God will only pour out as much of Himself as you are hungry for.

THE LAST FRONTIER

Are you hungry for the deep things of God? Are you hungry to receive God ideas? I am. I don't want to live the rest of my life on milk. I want strong meat.

It's time for us to remove every barrier, every limitation. God wants a glorious church without blemish, spot or wrinkle. And that means we have to remove all carnality. When all carnality is removed, Jesus can share whatever He wants to share. Whatever the Holy Ghost wants to share, He can share—because now He has vessels of honor fit for the Master's use to pour information into.

God not only wants us to be people of faith and people of the Word, but He also wants us to be holy people. The Bible says we are a **peculiar people** (1 Peter 2:9). That doesn't mean we're "weird." It means we're special, different, set apart. We should not live as the world lives. We ought to be different.

> **But as he which hath called you is holy, so be ye holy in all manner of conversation** [lifestyle]; **Because it is written, Be ye holy; for I am holy.**
>
> **1 Peter 1:15,16**

I believe that the Holy Spirit wants to reveal to us what He could not reveal to any other generation. He wants to reveal what has been hidden in the past. I believe we're a generation that can walk in a greater dimension of divine favor, of the blessing of God, of the wisdom of God, of the knowledge of God, than any other generation that's ever existed. But we have to be hungry for it. We have to get rid of our limitations if we are to receive the God ideas that the Holy Spirit has been sent to reveal to us.

ONLY TEN PERCENT

It's time for believers all over the world to tap into the mind of Christ. To have the mind of Christ is to function and operate in maximum potential. As believers, we have great potential, but we can't live up to it in our own strength.

Scientists tell us that, in the natural, most people use only about ten percent of their available intelligence. If we are not drawing on the Holy Spirit and on the mind of Christ, we are operating on only ten percent of our potential. Even geniuses, people with very high IQs, operate on only about twenty-five percent of their potential.

But what percentage of our potential would we operate on if we had the mind of Christ? The Bible says, **In** [Him] **are hid all the treasures of wisdom and knowledge** (Colossians 2:3).

ONE DROP OF WATER

The wisdom of the universe is in Christ. After all, He is the Creator. It all started with Him (John 1:1). Isaiah 40 says that He took one drop of water in the hollow of His hand and one piece of dust in the palm of His hand, and He comprehended the weight displacement of the planet before He ever spoke it into existence.

Using one drop of water, God weighed every body of water that would be on earth for the entire history of the planet. That means He had to take into consideration every drop of rain and every snowflake that would ever fall on earth. He had to consider oceans and rivers and lakes. He had to consider the effect of floods on the weight displacement of the earth.

Then, with a single grain of dust, He weighed all of the mountains. How much does a mountain weigh? How much does Mount Everest weigh? To us the weight of Mount Everest is incalculable, but God knows what it weighs down to the ounce. All of the super computers in the world will never see the day when they can compute that. But God computed it from a single grain of dust.

And the Bible tells us we have His mind! We have His Spirit residing within us to lead us into all truth! We have all of the treasures of wisdom and knowledge available to us.

We have the mind of Christ **and do hold the thoughts (feelings and purposes) of His heart** (1 Corinthians 2:16 AMP). When you operate in the mind of Christ, the Holy Spirit will give you the capacity to hold the very thoughts, the feelings and the purposes of the heart of God Himself. Talk about walking in success! When you know the heart of God, you're going to be successful. You're going to be prosperous when you have access to the very thoughts and intentions of God.

JUST A SIMPLE LITTLE SYSTEM

Let me give you a couple of examples from my own experience of how tapping into the mind of Christ will help you do something you do not, in the natural, know how to do.

Years ago, when I first went to work for Kenneth Copeland, he gave me the job of traveling with him and setting up the equipment, primarily the sound system, in the auditoriums where he was scheduled to preach. Now, I had just come out of a paint and body shop. I did not know anything about a traveling ministry, and I certainly didn't know anything about setting up a sound system. I didn't know anything about amplifiers except that they were supposed to amplify sound. But how to get one to work I did not know.

Brother Copeland didn't instruct me in how to set it up. He just said, "Here are the speakers. Here are the amplifiers. Here's the microphone. Set it up." Well, it shouldn't have been very complicated. It was just a simple little unit from Radio Shack. He carried it around in the back of a station wagon along with everything else he owned. But I had never worked with a sound system before.

So at the first meeting where I had to set up the sound system, I decided I would get a head start on things. I decided I would set up the sound system the night before the meeting so I would be sure to have everything working by 10:00 the next morning when Brother Copeland was scheduled to begin preaching.

I went to the hotel ballroom where the meeting was to be held, unpacked all the equipment, started plugging in this and plugging in that—of course not really having any idea what I was doing. And all I got out of that sound system was silence! No matter what I did, I couldn't get any sound out of it.

I sat up all night trying to figure out how to set up that sound system properly. I read the manuals but couldn't make heads or tails out of them. I plugged in everything that could be plugged in. I tapped the microphone and blew in it until I didn't have any breath left. But nothing worked.

Of course, I knew I couldn't go ask Brother Copeland how to set this sound system up, because he was praying. And he doesn't allow anyone to interrupt him when he's praying.

Well, I stayed in that ballroom until 8:00 in the morning, trying everything I could think of to make that sound system work. But it wouldn't. And I could just imagine Brother Copeland walking up at 10:00 in front of a crowd of people and saying into the microphone, "Let's open our Bibles..." without any sound coming out of the speakers.

And so, at 8:00 in the morning, after I had been up all night trying to figure this thing out, I finally prayed. I prayed and prayed and prayed. I said, "Father, I don't know what I'm doing. If anybody knows how to work a sound system, it's got to be You. You invented the thing, or at least You invented the materials it's made of. Please show me what I'm doing wrong."

And in a little while I did a little of this and a little of that—and suddenly sound came out. The sound system worked! Praise the Lord!

I had just enough time to run up to my room, take a shower, put on my suit and get back down to the ballroom before Brother Copeland came in. He hooked up his microphone, preached his sermon and never knew I'd been up all night trying to figure out how to set up the sound system. He didn't know I hadn't been able to get it to work until I finally prayed and tapped into the wisdom of God.

Of course, that's what I should have done in the first place. I could have saved myself from losing a night's sleep if I had prayed and asked for God's help *before* I had gotten into trouble instead of after! I know that's what Brother Copeland would have told me to do if I had asked him. And I know it because that's exactly what he did tell me the next time I had to repair some equipment that I didn't know anything about.

PARTS ARE PARTS

Shortly after we got home from that meeting, the copier in the ministry office broke down. Brother Copeland tried to make a copy of something, but the copier wouldn't work. So he said to me, "Jerry, repair that copier."

Now wait a minute, I thought, *I worked on cars, not copiers. I don't know anything about copiers.* So I came out of my little cubbyhole office where I was duplicating tapes and started to say, "Brother Copeland, I don't know...."

But he laid his hands right on my forehead and said, "You have the mind of Christ. Fix the copier. I'll see you tomorrow."

Well, all right, I said to myself, *I have the mind of Christ. I have the mind of Christ. But what would Christ do if He needed a copier? I don't know what I'm doing, but I'm confessing that I have the mind of Christ.*

So I got a screwdriver and a few other tools out of my car and started taking that copier apart. I didn't have any idea what I was looking for. If I had seen something that wasn't working, I wouldn't have known it was the part that wasn't working. If it was broken, I wouldn't have known it was broken. I didn't have any idea how to fix a copier, but I kept confessing, "I have the mind of Christ."

I just kept unscrewing this and undoing that and taking this off until I had parts all over the floor. I had so many parts on the floor, I had to be careful to remember where they had come from. I pulled that copier apart. And when I had it completely dissected, I looked at it and said, "Yep, that's a broken copier, all right."

So then I just started putting it all back together. I put it together, and lo and behold, it worked perfectly! But the catch was that I had parts left over. The copier was working perfectly, but I hadn't put back all of the parts that I'd taken out of it. I decided the manufacturer must have put too many parts in it.

I don't know to this day what I did to fix that copier, but it worked. And we didn't have to have it repaired again. Praise the Lord. It worked perfectly without some of its original parts. I don't even know what parts they were. I mean, parts are parts. Apparently, the manufacturer put too many parts in it, because that copier worked fine from then on without them.

If Jesus can reveal to someone how to fix a copier, don't you suppose He might have other knowledge that might be helpful to us in these last days? The deep things of God have been reserved for our generation. Being able to comprehend and grasp the purposes of God's heart is going to put us in position to experience the greatest prosperity and success the world has ever seen.

But, as I said before, this is not going to happen to every Christian, because not every Christian is hungry for it. Not every Christian will reach out in faith and seize the opportunity for it. Unfortunately, many Christians are satisfied with where they are. They're content to stay limited. But those who are hungry for the deep things of God will increase in the knowledge of Him in direct proportion to their hunger. When knowing all you can about God is your ultimate goal, as it was for Paul, you will seize every opportunity to know more of Him and to serve Him in a greater capacity.

CHAPTER 8

◆ ◆ ◆

PERCEIVE IT, DECLARE IT, LAY HOLD UPON IT

As I've said all along, I firmly believe that you and I, the believers of this present generation, are the church that God has been waiting for. More and more people of this generation of believers are hungry for God. They are serious about pressing into the things of God. They are people who will not accept limitations. They are ready to stretch out in faith to seize every opportunity God gives them for greater success and more effectual service.

I believe God has longed for a people like us who are not satisfied with where we are. He has longed for a people who are not satisfied with just what we've learned so far.

That's not to say that it hasn't been good up to now. It has been good, but I want more. I serve a God who's big enough to give me more than enough. Praise the Lord. I serve a big God, and I don't know everything He wants me to know about Him yet. I haven't yet seen everything He can do. I'm hungry for more. And I'm sure you are too, or you wouldn't have come this far in reading this book.

LONG ENOUGH ON THIS MOUNTAIN

I said in the last chapter that we can't seize our God-given opportunities unless we are willing to let go of our limitations. That's not something I just figured out. The Bible reveals that God wants us to remove every limitation. God wants us to stretch our faith to progress to the next level of what He wants us to have. God never wants us to get stuck on a plateau or settle for just what we've achieved so far.

At the beginning of the book of Deuteronomy, Moses told the children of Israel that God wanted to take them to the next level. God knew they had been where they were long enough.

> **On this side Jordan, in the land of Moab, began Moses to declare this law, saying, The Lord our God spake unto us in Horeb, saying, Ye have dwelt long enough in this mount.**
>
> **Deuteronomy 1:5,6**

Now, I believe God is saying to the body of Christ right now, "You have dwelt long enough on this mountain." Even though we've had some wonderful blessings on this mountain and have seen God do marvelous things on this side of Jordan, we've been here long enough.

I believe God is saying to each of us, "You've been at the place where you are in your personal life long enough. It's time to move on. You can't get comfortable where you are. You can't relax your faith. Even if you've just had a major victory in your life, this is not the time to take a spiritual vacation.

"But, Brother Jerry, can't we have a little break before we have to believe God again?" No, you cannot. Time is short. Time is running out, and God is holding our generation responsible for some big faith projects.

My wife sometimes says, "Jerry, can't we please finish one project before we start another?" The more I hang around God, the more faith projects I become pregnant with. I'm pregnant with a litter of faith projects. I have a litter of faith projects inside of my spirit waiting to be born.

Never One Like This

God says, **Ye have dwelt long enough in this mount.** You've been where you are long enough. It's time to stretch. It's time to go past where you are now. Some of you reading this book have already gone way beyond what your parents thought you could do. Some of you have broken the mold. I like to say, "There has never been a Savelle in the Savelle family like me. I broke the mold." I've gone further. I have gone beyond what any of my ancestors did. I don't think the way they thought. I don't live the way they lived. I went beyond. I said, "This family has been on this mountain long enough. It's time to go higher."

Not Without Opposition

However, we are not going to get to the next level without having to overcome opposition. When God told the children of Israel to leave where they were and go to the next level, He sent them directly toward their adversaries.

> **Turn you, and take your journey, and go to the mount of the Amorites, and unto all the places nigh thereunto, in the plain, in the hills, and in the vale, and in the south, and by the sea side, to the land of the Canaanites,**

125

and unto Lebanon, unto the great river, the river Euphrates. Behold, I have set the land before you: go in and possess the land which the Lord sware unto your fathers, Abraham, Isaac, and Jacob, to give unto them and to their seed after them.

And I spake unto you at that time, saying, I am not able to bear you myself alone: The Lord your God hath multiplied you, and, behold, ye are this day as the stars of heaven for multitude. (The Lord God of your fathers make you a thousand times so many more as ye are, and bless you, as he hath promised you!)

Deuteronomy 1:7-11

The trouble with many Christians today, the reason they don't grow up spiritually, is that they want a comfortable Christianity. They want to go to the next level, but they don't want any opposition. They don't want any pressure. They seem to have the mistaken idea that if something is God's will, it will be easy to accomplish. Well, if that's true, I've never been in the will of God!

I'm particularly fond of a statement made by the radio commentator Paul Harvey. He said, "You can always tell when you're on the road to success, because it's usually uphill all the way."

TAKE PLEASURE IN REPROACHES

We've already seen that the apostle Paul had to overcome the adversaries that came along with his opportunity to preach the gospel in Ephesus (1 Corinthians 16:9). If you read Paul's letters carefully, you will see that every step of the way he was confronted with opposition. I call him "the apostle of confrontation." He was constantly in a faith fight with adversaries. But he got to the point that he thrived on confronting opposition.

He said, **I take pleasure...in reproaches** (2 Corinthians 12:10). In other words, Paul was saying, "I love a good fight."

"LOOK, THERE IT IS!"

God told the Israelites to go to the mount of the Amorites because **Behold, I have set the land before you: go in and possess the land which the Lord sware unto your fathers, Abraham, Isaac, and Jacob, to give unto them and to their seed after them** (Deuteronomy 1:8).

Now notice that God was saying to the Israelites, "There's something up ahead that I ordained for you to have. Go forward and take possession of it." God has ordained things up ahead that belong to you and me. But the only way we will ever lay our hands upon them is to get off of the mountain that we've been on so long.

When God gives us an opportunity, He says to us, in effect, "There's your opportunity. There's the vision I want you to lay hold of. Go take possession of it, suddenly and by force."

Do you remember what we said at the beginning of this book about the necessity of perceiving, of recognizing, your opportunity? Many people miss opportunities because they are insensitive to them. They aren't paying attention when God says, "There it is. Go get it." And opportunities don't wait around for the faint-hearted or the slow-to-move. God said to the Israelites, "Look, there's the land that I promised you. Now go up and possess it, suddenly and by force."

Step 1: Perceive It

The first step in the process of seizing any opportunity is *to perceive or to see it*. Before you can lay hold of an opportunity, you must have a vision, a concept, of what God is calling you to do. You must see a cause that is bigger than yourself.

Someone once asked Helen Keller, "What would you say is worse than being blind?" And she answered immediately, "Having no vision." What a powerful statement. Helen Keller understood the importance of having an inner vision. Even though she couldn't see physically, she had a vision. And her vision touched the world and became an inspiration to thousands of people.

Do you realize that inside of you is the creative ability of God? The vision God has placed, or wants to place, inside of you has the potential to change the world.

"You mean inside little old me, Brother Jerry?" Yes, I mean inside little old you. Who would have thought that a blind girl like Helen Keller would touch the world with her story? And you too have a story that the world is waiting for. Inside you God has placed a vision that has the potential to change the world.

Learning To Stretch

You have to be willing to perceive that God-given vision and to reach out for it by faith. You have to learn to get off of the comfortable plateau you've been on and stretch your faith to go to the next level. Every person, spiritual and unspiritual, who has ever achieved anything great has had to learn to stretch. You don't achieve great things without stretching yourself to reach further than you ever have before. If you are going to bring your vision into reality, you have to be willing to stretch.

As we've already said, one of the major reasons people refuse to stretch is the fear of failure. Or we might call it the "fear of the unknown." The worst question you can ask when God directs you to step out in faith is "What if...?" You should make an effort to remove that phrase from your vocabulary.

There is no "what if..." when you serve an unlimited God. There is no "what if..." when you serve a covenant-keeping God. Thinking about "what if..." will keep you on the plateau that has limited you. To grow in the things of God, you have to get off of the plateau of "what if...."

To move forward to seize our opportunities, each of us must fully discover and tap into the potential God says is ours in Christ.

Ready for Anything

In Philippians 4:13, Paul said, **I can do all things through Christ which strengtheneth me.** *The Amplified Bible* says it this way:

> **I have strength for all things in Christ Who empowers me [I am ready for anything and equal to anything through Him Who infuses inner strength into me; I am self-sufficient in Christ's sufficiency.]**

Paul is saying that when you begin to tap into your full potential in Christ, you are then able to say, "I am ready for anything." And not only that, but you can declare your readiness by faith and have complete confidence and deep conviction when you declare it. You can say, "I am equal to anything Satan can throw in front of me. Hallelujah!"

When you see in your spirit the vision God has called you to accomplish and you tap into the mind of Christ and the strength of Christ within you, you cannot be defeated. It is impossible for you to be defeated when you tap into the spirit of might, which comes into your life through Christ, the anointed One.

Breaking the Old Records

When I was a kid, I enjoyed Tarzan movies. A number of actors have played the role of Tarzan, but my favorite was Johnny Weismuller. Fifty years ago, Johnny Weismuller was an Olympic swimmer. At that time, he held many world titles in swimming. In the thirties and forties, he was considered the greatest swimmer in the world.

But today, thirteen-year-old boys and girls are breaking Johnny Weismuller's records every day! Just like the successors of Roger Bannister, the runner who first broke the four-minute mile barrier, they are not satisfied with what an older generation of athletes was able to achieve. They are tapping into a greater potential and breaking records every day. They have seen a vision of what's ahead, and they are pressing toward it.

It's the same with the church. What the church couldn't accomplish fifty years ago, we are accomplishing. What barriers they couldn't break, we break every day. Every morning when we wake and say, "Praise God! Another day to live for Jesus. Another day to stand on the Word of God. Another day to walk by faith and not by sight"—we break records that the church only dreamed of breaking fifty years ago.

But it takes vision to press forward to break these records. Therefore, the first step in seizing your God-given opportunity is *to see it.*

THE PRIMARY DIFFERENCE

The primary difference between successful people and unsuccessful people, either in the secular or the spiritual realm, is that *successful people are motivated by vision.* They see what they're pressing toward inside of them. They're motivated by something they see. They have a dream that is bigger than themselves.

Your dream has to be bigger than you. If it's not bigger than you, it won't take any faith to accomplish it.

And your dream has to be something you see ahead of you. Successful people believe in something that is just beyond their reach. If you can accomplish your vision without faith, then it's questionable whether it's really God-inspired, because everything God tells you to do is impossible.

God doesn't call you to do things you can do by yourself. God's projects always require faith because the Bible says it's impossible to please Him without faith (Hebrews 11:6). Everything God calls you to do is beyond your reach, beyond your resources, beyond your ability. But Christ strengthens you, empowers you and infuses into you His ability.

With Christ's ability you can reach further because you're no longer limited to yourself. You have the spirit of might and the anointing of the anointed One in you and on you to bring what looked impossible into the realm of the possible.

But in order to receive Christ's empowerment, you must perceive and grasp a vision, a dream, that is beyond your reach in the natural. And you also have to become deeply convicted and convinced that if you are persistent, you will eventually grasp what was at first unreachable. You will eventually attain it. You will eventually possess your promised land.

No Looking Back

Remember what the apostle Paul said in his letter to the Philippians:

> **Brethren, I count not myself to have apprehended: but this one thing I do, forgetting those things which are behind, and reaching forth unto those things which are before, I press toward the mark for the prize of the high calling of God in Christ Jesus.**

> **Philippians 3:13,14**

Notice particularly that Paul says, "I forget the things behind, and I reach forth and press toward my goal." *The Amplified Bible* says, **forgetting what lies behind and straining forward to what lies ahead.** Paul was always straining forward to what lay ahead of him.

You should be aware that in the natural, straining forward causes you to be a little off balance. If he sees you off balance, the devil may think he can defeat you by tripping you up as you lean forward and press toward your goal. But when your foundation is the Word, even when you feel a little off balance, you cannot be tripped up. God says, "Even if you stumble and fall, I will not allow you to be utterly cast down."

Paul was motivated by something he couldn't quite reach in the natural. He was motivated by something he saw inside of him. He could see his dream in the distance, and it motivated him to keep pressing on. You can never stop pressing. The only way to win is by pressing and straining forward to grasp what's beyond your reach.

BURNING YOUR BRIDGES

In Luke 9:62, Jesus warned His disciples, **No man, having put his hand to the plough, and looking back, is fit for the kingdom of God.** People who don't keep pressing are not fit for the kingdom of God. People who are prone to quit are not fit. People who give up easily under pressure are not fit. If you're looking for a comfortable Christianity, you aren't fit.

After he has put his hand to the plow, no man can keep looking back to the things behind. You have to burn your bridges behind you. You can't keep looking back. There's no security there. You left that place. Now you're headed for the unknown. But in your spirit you know that God has given you a dream. In your spirit you can see your promised land ahead, and you keep pressing toward it.

NEVER TOO LATE

It's never too late to pursue a God-given dream or to seize a God-given opportunity.

Moses was eighty years old when he became a deliverer. Caleb was eighty-five when he said, "Give me this mountain." More recently, it is said that the preacher John

Wesley rode horseback all over England preaching the gospel until he was eighty-eight years old. Thomas Edison was eight-five when he invented the mimeograph machine. Colonel Sanders was seventy when he invented "finger-lickin' good" chicken. Casey Stengel became manager of the New York Yankees baseball team when he was seventy-five years old.

What motivates men like this? What is the common thread that runs through their success in both the spiritual and the secular realms? The common thread is that they never quit pressing. They never gave up on their God-given dreams.

It's never too late to achieve a God-given dream. But if we're going to experience what God wants us to experience in these last days, we're going to have to see it first.

Proverbs 29:18 says, **Where there is no vision, the people perish.** Vision gives you a purpose and a cause for getting up every morning. Every person must have a cause, a vision, to motivate him or her to fight for what we're entitled to in God.

"Is There Not a Cause?"

There must be a cause in your life that you're willing to stretch yourself for, to be ridiculed for, to be criticized for. You won't be able to press into your cause, your dream, without experiencing criticism from others who don't understand the cause.

David had to overcome criticism and ridicule before he could press in to his God-given vision. When he first arrived at the Israelite camp and was shocked to see his brothers and the rest of the men of Israel running away from Goliath, he saw an opportunity to take up the cause himself. However, his brothers just laughed at him and accused him of being a show-off:

> And David spake to the men that stood by him, saying, What shall be done to the man that killeth this Philistine, and taketh away the reproach from Israel? for who is this uncircumcised Philistine, that he should defy the armies of the living God? And the people answered him after this manner, saying, So shall it be done to the man that killeth him. And Eliab his eldest brother heard when he spake unto the men; and Eliab's anger was kindled against David, and he said, Why camest thou down hither? and with whom hast thou left those few sheep in the wilderness? I know thy pride, and the naughtiness of thine heart; for thou art come down that thou mightest see the battle. And David said, What have I now done? Is there not a cause?
>
> 1 Samuel 17:26-29

Take particular note of what Eliab said. **I know thy pride, and the naughtiness of thine heart....** He was accusing David of leaving his father's sheep unguarded just to watch the battle. But **David said, ...Is there not a cause?** David was saying, "No, I'm here because there is a cause, a need."

People with a cause see something other people can't see.

Step 2: Declare It

Not only do people with a cause see something other people can't see, but they are bold to *declare* what they see. They are bold to *say* what God has called them to do. And people like Eliab mistake these faith declarations for pride and boasting.

Not only will people mistake your faith for pride and your faith confessions for boasting, but they will immediately try to convince you that you are not able. Just like David, you'll suddenly be surrounded by people who say, **Thou art not able.**

> **And David said to Saul, Let no man's heart fail because of him; thy servant will go and fight with this Philistine. And Saul said to David, Thou art not able to go against this Philistine to fight with him: for thou art but a youth, and he a man of war from his youth. And David said unto Saul, Thy servant kept his father's sheep, and there came a lion, and a bear, and took a lamb out of the flock: And I went out after him, and smote him, and delivered it out of his mouth: and when he arose against me, I caught him by his beard, and smote him, and slew him. Thy servant slew both the lion and the bear: and this uncircumcised Philistine shall be as one of them, seeing he hath defied the armies of the living God. David said moreover, The Lord that delivered me out of the paw of the lion, and out of the paw of the bear, he will deliver me out of the hand of this Philistine. And Saul said unto David, Go, and the Lord be with thee.**
>
> **1 Samuel 17:32-37**

Have you ever noticed that when you start a faith project, some relatives and friends gather around like vultures, saying, **Thou art not able?** "Who do you think you are? You're just trying to be better than the rest of the family. You think you're better than we are. We know your pride." The people you thought would be on your side want to tie you down and keep you scratching away with the chickens in the barnyard when you're ready to soar with the eagles.

When David went to King Saul, who was a mighty man of valor himself, King Saul said, "Well, you're just a kid. You can't fight this giant." You would think a man of valor would want to encourage a young man to be a man of valor, too. Instead, Saul tried to discourage him.

BOLDLY DECLARE

But David refused to be discouraged. He had seen his cause, and he recognized the importance of boldly declaring his faith. You see, once you have identified your vision, it's important that you declare it, that you say it, that you affirm it—not only to yourself, but also in public whenever it's necessary. Don't be bashful about declaring your cause. David not only saw himself slaying Goliath, but he boldly declared he would do it.

He said, "this uncircumcised Philistine will not be any different than the lion or the bear. God delivered the lion and the bear into my hands, and He will deliver this uncircumcised Philistine into my hand also." David boldly spoke his faith in his God.

Second Corinthians 4:13 says faith will speak what it believes. **We having the same spirit of faith, according as it is written, I believed, and therefore have I**

spoken; we also believe, and therefore speak. The spirit of faith constantly speaks what it believes. The biblical way to victory is first to *perceive* it, then to *declare* it and finally, to *lay hold upon* it.

STEP 3: LAY HOLD UPON IT

The third step in seizing your God-given opportunity is to *lay hold upon it.* Don't hang around waiting for something to happen. Lay hold on your dream. Your opportunity is not just going to come to you. You have to go to it.

That's exactly what David did. David saw himself slaying Goliath. He decreed he would slay Goliath. And then he went out to seize his opportunity. The Bible says he hastened. He ran toward the giant.

And it came to pass, when the Philistine arose, and came and drew nigh to meet David, that David hasted, and ran toward the army to meet the Philistine. And David put his hand in his bag, and took thence a stone, and slang it, and smote the Philistine in his forehead, that the stone sunk into his forehead; and he fell upon his face to the earth. So David prevailed over the Philistine with a sling and with a stone, and smote the Philistine, and slew him; but there was no sword in the hand of David.

1 Samuel 17:48-50

When, like David, you see a cause, when you have a vision you see deeply in your spirit, when you begin to decree it—then you must go forward and lay hold upon it.

God wants us to dream bigger dreams than we've ever dreamed before. This is not the time to abort our dreams. It's the time to recapture the dream of God and pursue it and possess it, suddenly and by force.

I believe God is challenging believers right now to stretch, to expand, to grow. These are days of supernatural increase. There's never been a better time for us to be successful than right now. There's never been a better time for us to be prosperous than right now. There's never been a better time for us to achieve better things in our lives than right now.

I challenge you today to seize your God-given opportunity by faith. I challenge you to perceive it, declare it, lay hold upon it. And then, regardless of the difficulties, regardless of the adversity and the adversaries, regardless of the criticism and the persecution and the ridicule, persevere until you have accomplished all that God has called you to accomplish.

ABOUT THE AUTHOR

Dr. **Jerry Savelle** is a noted author, evangelist and teacher who travels extensively throughout the United States, Canada and around the globe. He is president of Jerry Savelle Ministries International, a ministry of many outreaches devoted to meeting the needs of believers all over the world.

Well-known for his balanced biblical teaching, Dr. Savelle has conducted seminars, crusades and conventions for over twenty-five years as well as ministering in thousands of churches and fellowships. He is in great demand today because of his inspiring message of victory and faith and his vivid, and often humorous, illustrations from the Bible. He teaches the uncompromising Word of God with a power and an authority that is exciting, but with a love that delivers the message directly to the spirit man.

In addition to his international headquarters in Crowley, Texas, Dr. Savelle is also founder of JSMI-Kenya; JSMI-United Kingdom; JSMI-South Africa; JSMI-Australia; and JSMI-Tanzania. In 1994, he established the JSMI Bible Institute and School of World Evangelism. It is a two-year school for the preparation of ministers to take the gospel of Jesus Christ to the nations of the world.

The missions outreach of his ministry extends to over fifty countries around the world. JSMI further ministers the Word of God through its prison ministry outreach.

Dr. Savelle has authored many books and has an extensive video and cassette teaching tape ministry and a worldwide television broadcast. Thousands of books, tapes and videos are distributed around the world each year through Jerry Savelle Ministries International.

To contact Jerry Savelle,
write:

Jerry Savelle
P. O. Box 748
Crowley, Texas 76036

*Please include your prayer requests
and comments when you write.*

OTHER BOOKS BY JERRY SAVELLE

Are You Tired of Sowing Much?
Force of Joy
Honoring Your Heritage of Faith
If Satan Can't Steal Your Joy
Right Mental Attitude
Sharing Jesus Effectively
The Established Heart
Turning Your Adversity Into Victory
You Can Have Abundant Life

Available from your local bookstore.

HARRISON HOUSE
Tulsa, Oklahoma 74153

THE HARRISON HOUSE VISION

Proclaiming the truth and the power
of the Gospel of Jesus Christ
with excellence;
Challenging Christians to
Live victoriously,
Grow spiritually,
Know God intimately.